EXCEPTIONAL

DEVELOPING THE GLOBAL BEST

DR. ROBERT SCOTT

ISBN 978-0-9847119-4-9
TALENTYPES.COM
© 2016 ROBERT SCOTT

**You have to learn the rules of the game
and then you have to play better than anyone else**

— Einstein

TABLE OF CONTENTS

Aptitude 5

Clarity. 19

Accuracy 27

Excellence 35

Confident 53

Priority 61

Persistent 71

Achievement 81

APTITUDE

"EXCEPTIONAL!" ... SCREAMED THE PRESIDENT of a national food company as my golf ball soared from several hundred feet away like a line drive hitting the top of the pin only to drop straight into the hole; my foursome jumping up and down; cheering. Not being any type of sports fan and only involved in this golf tournament for purely business reasons, I thought my freak shot of the century was exactly that and nothing that reflected any level of skill. However this celebratory pathology went on for the entire day and that evening at the tournament dinner I even received some type of award which I politely waited until returning home to quietly throw away as not to offend anyone. The question that kept spinning in my head, was how anyone could believe that this once in a lifetime event that I would never duplicate again was anything close to being legitimately regarded as Exceptional.

Exceptional confers an element of Aptitude and Achievement; neither were present in this freakish event. A more accurate description could be found in the words of one of my students who said " What you did today is exception." Indeed, he was correct. Jack, having attended a small community college part time for three years, had a collection of courses that cost him virtually nothing due to his financial situation the institution waived the fee. Noting his aptitude, I continually encouraged him to step up into a four year program. Finally, he applied and with some relational assistance he was admitted to the university. The question became how much of this prior work would they accept.

In planning for the meeting, I mapped out a strategy to link the courses to his professional experience and thereby demonstrating proficiency of the subject matter. For over an hour we met as I built my case and connected the dots. The administrator asked Jack many questions to demonstrate subject mastery. He hit the ball out of the park every time as we had rehearsed this most important meeting of his life for well over a month. As a result of this all important meeting, the school would admit him as a second semester sophomore. In a little more than an hour, we had saved him more that thirty thousand dollars in tuition cost. I count this day as one of the best ones of my entire life and, yes, our mutual accomplishment satisfies my definition of something that is exceptional. The key element that makes it different from the freakish golf shot is that I had the aptitude and skills to repeat this achievement again. This Aptitude was a combination of Natural Talent and Learned Talent that would only be further perfected with additional experience.

Still more puzzling are purely Natural Talents that have a life of their own, comparable to an iceberg, you only see the conscious demonstration of their power; more than two thirds of it is unconscious and beyond your ability to explain.

"What an Exceptional gift you have", said the CEO of an international manufacturing corporation. The last six plus hours we spent together on a flight was something else and I always tell myself after one of these experiences; the next time I'm not going to say anything.

I took my seat on the plane and luckily no one sat in the middle, which is a great relief to most travelers. On the inside was a very professional looking man who had the Ivy League patina; it is their badge of privilege that's worn on their sleeve. As we were ready for take-off he half pursed his lips as a polite greeting. As I caught his eye, his karma instantly flashed into my head. Into the wild blue yonder we proceeded and the feeling that I captured left me with a most unsettled sensation. He was blindly looking out the window and as I glanced his way he look at me again. Some time passed until all of the dots were connected in my head. The usual internal wrestling was now underway.

The question is always one of pastoring and helping versus disturbing and making it worse. As this was many years ago and the pathology of our insanely politically correct society had no bearing on my decision making process, with a bright smile I caught his eye and said, " Excuse me, I can help?"

With that came the disclosure of my complete perception of his family situation along with a short resume of who, what and where. The prophetic gift took his breath away as I hit his concern spot on. The man became weepy and all I could think was, " Oh brother – what did you get yourself into?" I reached out and held his hand and told him that it would all work out. He then went into a three hours therapy session with the most articulate descriptions of all the dynamics which I absorbed like a sponge. At the end of this endless soliloquy I was spent and told him that I needed to sleep.

An hour later I awoke and with great anticipation the man asked me, "What's the answer?" By the end of the flight the man was laughing and joking with me, as the large burden had been lifted and a path forward had been found. We parted at the airport never to directly speak again but instead to have an email relationship, in which he reveals snapshots of my advice which he executed that positively changed the direction of his life. Still more mystical, is this bond our mile high experience had created. On those several occasions when, out of the blue this man comes into my head, it only means one thing; he's visiting the area where I live. My email to confirm this fact only further adds more wonder to this man, who is astonished by something that I have absolutely no ability to explain.

This type of Bestowed Talent is the most Exceptional, but is not as predictive as the Learned Talent, as the course of its energies are not within your complete grasp to channel or control. All one can do is to flexibly dance with this gift and not waste a lot of time being introspective and looking for some great cosmic meaning.

As I consider the subject of what actually being Exceptional is all about such a flood of memories fills my mind. So many diverse people who have all exhibited aspects of genius talent in these small micro-behaviors, but, who are burdened with great deficits in other areas that cloud those gifts considerably. My task is to amplify those gifts and teach them to self - regulate the deficits in order to rise and become strong.

So what is it to be Exceptional?

Being a spiritual person, everything begins with the natural gifts that were given to us on the day of our birth and our life-long obligation to fulfill their destiny. Each person receives a Bestowed Talent that, by Divine Order, will be their contribution in the salvation of humanity. Due to our Free Will, it's completely up to us to elect whether we choose to use it or lose it. The entire mystical wonder of it all comes down to how we perfect that spirit energy inside us.

Aptitude plays such a very large part in being Exceptional as it is our ability to rapidly learn and integrate new skills. This experiential imprinting begins Day One on the planet, as life is nothing more than an accumulation of sensations and experiences that reveal, grow and define us. There are two schools of thought here that I have wrestled with since I was a child.

On the one hand, the American Approach was that many experiences, both good and bad were great teachers. In fact even if you had many bad experiences, this was still positive, as suffering through the negative results it taught you what not to do. The challenge I've always had with this is in all of the emotional scarring such experiences produced obviously has a significant impact on all of your internal wiring. I'm not a advocate for the stick, as I much prefer the carrot.

Yet I know this is a prevailing thought in the American psyche. In fact, once when I was bringing a gubernatorial candidate to meet people around the county, I met a long-time teacher and friend on the main street that I had not seen for quite some time. Coming from my overly affectionate sub-culture, where we kiss everyone, my joy brimmed over as I hugged and kissed her. My old Yankee candidate was uncomfortable by this and said sarcastically " I guess you really like the people here?" My response, " We believe it is better to be loved than to be feared. Our influence is founded on kindness not power."

He told me "For a man of your age you are foolish and have so much to learn." I smiled and continued my tour, knowing he was going to lose the election in a big way. With thirty percent of the vote, my perception was proven correct.

My old Brahmin echoed a very retro concept, which assured us that by negative reinforcement we could attain positive results. I never quite got this, as it did nothing to satisfy the energies of the heart which directs the course of love and life. These ideas are completely alien to the manner of my upbringing.

Long before we had "Helicopter Parents" the concept of the Archetypal Parent was part and parcel of so many subcultures in America. Granted, they were not texting and in your business 365 24/7. As their Unconditional Love was a telepathic energy that sat in your pocket every day. They did not ascribe to the American Approach of bad experiences being good teachers. Their task was to shield you from all negative experience until you reached maturity emerging as a kind of "Ubermensch" who was not merely intelligent, but a complete, emotionally integrated individual.

Some may say that we were babied and coddled but the fact remains in only two generations these sub-cultures went from the bottom of the pecking order to the top in less than fifty years. Along with this prolific rise came a generation of individuals who were the best in show, the top in their field and raised the bar of excellence even higher. However, for the intellectual qualities that create Exceptional individuals to remain sustainable, there must exist a Community of Purpose which continually refreshes these hard working and driven people.

Because the fulfillment of all these personal needs becomes an unconscious and inherent part of life, the individual must devote all of their energies into engaging their Aptitude and the further development of their Emotional Intelligence.

Kyle, one of my students came from intense rural poverty, yet was extremely talented using his hands. His extended family had worked in the factories for generations. After securing admission to a school in the city, we went to a Thai Restaurant. Kyle had never been to such a place and did not even know what chop sticks were. When the food arrived I began to eat with the chop sticks. He wanted to do the same and asked me to demonstrate. I gave a quick ten second lesson. With great dexterity he picked them up and started using them as if he had been eating with chop sticks his entire life. His tactile gift was exceptional yet the deficiency of his social and emotional life made it impossible for him to ever advance. He lasted only one semester in college, as the emotional internal wiring for him to self regulate and direct his energies were completely beyond his grasp. All of my Exceptional Students (who) I write about in this book, may have come from poverty, but at their core had this unconditionally loving Archetypal Parent figure who helped contain their youthful impulsiveness, within specific boundaries until they emerged with the maturity of an "Ubermensch".

It was this Yankee Stoicism, the Puritan Work Ethic and the ardent talents of various ethnic sub-culture's which created American Exceptionalism. The great melting pot that further launched this was Universal Education; today's Public School Systems. This became the avenue of opportunity and advancement. These two words defined the very essence of the Old School Spirit that produced the American Century.

Being Exceptional has become a code word for some kind of privilege that our politically correct society delights in attempting to both over regulate and extinguish. In previous times Exceptionalism was the central ideal of our national culture. The present revolt by the voters in America is a re-adjustment away from the failed policies that seek to diminish the influence of merit while encouraging dependent entitlement.

Exceptionalism more than just a cultural philosophy, it is a lifestyle of developing Aptitude within a process of further advancing Collective Achievement.

Achievement is an act of accomplishment through the combined actions of Talent, Practice, Exertion and my favorite Perseverance.

The key factor is having the opportunity to be immersed within a Community of Purpose which serves as a Collective Intelligence that seeks to advance the objective of Achievement. Over the last twenty years, I have seen the continual closing of that Opportunity Window, through sky rocketing educational cost and (disproportional) privilege given to certain special interest groups.

I look at two cousins who were both my students. One of them from fifteen years ago, possessed a strong aptitude and moderate work ethic, but had an absence of vision. He graduated from university with a small amount of student debt, great skills and an unlimited amount of career opportunities. He advanced on to a entry level position where he has preformed exceptionally well. Lucky for him that fifteen years ago, the prevailing climate provided the luxury of years to get his act together and climb the learning curve.

His cousin's world is far different. This student is wonderfully talented, with a great work ethic and knows what he wants to do. However his college admission required more effort to secure. He will graduate with five times the amount of student debt and more than a line of employers waiting to offer him a position. He is going to create his own business. He is clearly is much more Exceptional than his cousin in many attributes, but the external conditions that are the Rules of his Game are far more complex and unforgiving in the present age.

The #1 Principal in becoming Exceptional is knowing the Rules of the Game and the Arena where it will be played out... even the gifted must plan their next move into the future!

All of these observations are merely the external behaviors of something much deeper going on in your mind. So let's pop the hood and look at the engine that's propelling this Exceptional vehicle.

INNER WISDOM — THE ESSENTIAL SELF

This is where everything begins, in this crucible of the mind where we construct the image of who we are or even more importantly who we desire to become. In essence, we are what we are becoming. So the starting place of being Exceptional is in the standards and constructs that are the Frameworks of your Life. These Frameworks are the results of all the cumulative experiences as previously mentioned. It is difficult for me to believe that if these Frameworks are cluttered with an abundance of negative ions, that the wiring is going to be as effective as if there was absolutely no clutter at all. These Frameworks are the nuts and bolts of your Critical Thinking skills. While we readily see the conscious side of our Critical Thinking ability, we have virtually no perception of the unconscious realm which is strongly influenced by our Emotional Intelligence.

This Emotional Intelligence is the keystone for anything that is Exceptional as it is your Inner Wisdom which when put to the test, rises in both its Audacity and Tenacity to prevail and win!

So, long before you do one thing that could be considered Exceptional, let alone become an integrated Exceptional individual, you have to possess a rock solid image of who you are, what you believe and what is the destiny that your seek to fulfill. ..Sorry… you can't Construct the Exceptional House without building a more Exceptional Foundation.

INTRINSIC ENERGY — CREATIVE MANIFESTATION

Once you have the psychic foundation in place, free from internal distractions that disrupt your inner circuitry, all of your instinctive energy is ready to make its mark upon the world. Here lies the impetus, the spark in your mind that wakes each morning and feels compelled to create a masterpiece of everything in which it is employed. When that Intrinsic Energy is paired with the standards of the your Inner Wisdom, watch out; something amazing is going to happen. This is where many people fail, as they are not introspective, taking the time to know themselves, or make peace with themselves. Unless you have the Frameworks of Life in place, there can be no consistent plan of execution.… To be Exceptional is To be Persistent.

ALPHA ATTRIBUTES — PRIMARY MOTIVATION

With both Inner Wisdom and Intrinsic Energy we journey into the mystical realm of the psyche which is vast and still not completely explored. We attempt to reveal and explain much of its inner workings as the driving energy motivates behavior. If we are fortunate and wise we have aligned all of the cosmic forces within the psyche, to develop our own personal relationship and balance with it. This equilibrium is an essential factor in your ability to successfully execute the Frameworks of your Life Plan, which takes many decades of sustained intensity to achieve. Yes, being Exceptional is not for the weak of heart. It is a lot of hard work.

One of the reasons that these ethnic sub-groups produce so many Exceptional individuals is the cultural structures, the many mores and values which become the framework of everyday life. This, in turn, imprints cumulative layers of behavior which instill a tremendous amount of self-discipline and direction. So, for them, the long hard road to Exceptionalism is far less arduous as it is the only lifestyle that they have ever known. Curiously, all of the people who exist in their circles manifest the same behaviors.

So, these seven Alpha Attributes which are the ingredients that make this Exceptional Stew, are not seen as unusual behaviors but essential to living a productive life. In fact, people that do not manifest them are actually viewed as not being completely developed. These more traditional cultures reward these behaviors of excellence and cast a dim view of the more modern lifestyle philosophy of "if it feels good do it."

Once when we were in Bahrain, having dinner with a member of the ruling family his daughter voiced her opinion about the inappropriateness of a certain music video. Later, one of my team members told me that she was too uptight and out of touch with the world . I explained, that in our culture, there is freedom to express ourselves how we please and that we put very little value on self discipline. In their culture they view this as the easy way out and a weakness of spirit. To them, the successful individual does not live for momentary pleasure, but constructs a comprehensive lifestyle in which their consistent good behavior produces sustained successes in the context of a community with a defined purpose.

Of course, there are eccentric geniuses who naturally have all seven Alpha Attributes but even as I researched all of them, their behavior was outlandish, though each was possessed of a core value of hard work and persistence. This tells me that anyone can achieve the proficiency of having all seven Alpha Attributes but must invest in themselves and be willing to give some things up in their life to accomplish that objective.

BETA BEHAVIORS — YOUR OPERATING SYSTEM

Better than naming of all of the Beta Behaviors, the take-away here are the terms and conditions of what you need to create them; for each is a part of a cumulative process in becoming Exceptional.

The Inner Wisdom frames the structure for the Intrinsic Energy that constructs the seven Alpha Attributes which manifest themselves in about twenty Beta Behaviors. This is Your Operating System, an consider it manual that keeps you on track. More than an arduous goal for the Exceptional individuals that I have met, it is a hard-wired part of their daily lifestyle, it is who they are. For other it who they want to become.

I had a student, Carol who was intellectually gifted but extremely introversive, though she earnestly sought to overcome this impediment. She began by observing the behavior of the leaders in her peer group. Slowly, she amassed a grocery list of attributes / behaviors to emulate. Carol was relentless in her pursuit, with a level of forbearance that was truly inspiring . For about five years we met several times a month and with the passage of time her efforts resulted in a most beautiful swan. Through sheer determination she re-wired her internal circuits to the point that twenty years later she is a completely different individual. Granted her situation is most unusual, but even on a more micro level it proves that Learned Behavior can become just as effective as Natural Ability.

She is an Exceptional attorney, tops in her field but when asked if all of these Elements of Self come any easier twenty years later; her answer was most surprising. These extroversive behaviors are never an unconscious response but consciously configured through the actions of her will power. Gone is the former anxiety that debilitated her, as there is a constant vigilance that never allows her unconscious tendencies to take control.

Carol is very aware that her consistent behavior forms the framework of her Lifestyle Culture which becomes the foundation of her reputation. This solid reputation, as time proceeds, is observed by others as her consistent, dependable Personal Brand. The old adage is correct, if you keep doing all the small things right every day, eventually you become excellent at everything that you do. The critical factor in becoming Exceptional is that you cannot just correctly achieve fifty percent of the time but must strive to accomplish tasks at the best level you can, at every opportunity. Doing so is what makes Carol such a Super Star!

UNIQUE BRAND — CULTURE OF EXCEPTIONALISM

Carol's inspiring story is the epic of the human spirit, forever seeking to rise. It is an essential part of our DNA , along with our great impetus to be a source of creation. One of my greatest concerns, in our present Politically Correct Age is the popular consternation created by the idea that all people are not going to be equal. Some people from Bestowed Talents and others, like Carol from hard won Learned Behaviors, are going to be the cream that rises to the top. Achievement / Merit are created through the individual's investment of their time and resources. The ancient philosopher got it right when he said, "In order to achieve something special you must give up something of personal value (your time or leisure) or delay the enjoyment of these things to a later time."

So, this idea that we all can become like a fungible jar of bean is insane and ignores millenniums of history and civilization. Each individual possesses a Unique Brand and their destiny to take that portion of energy and develop their own personal process to grow/ improve it to its most optimal state of significance. Within the dynamic of this Creativity Impetus Gene that is a fundamental building block in our DNA comes the merit /recognition that achievement produces.

We are all Exceptional in some unique way but the secret to a valuable amplification of this inborn characteristics is found in expanding the dimensions of that specific gift, to have the maximum amount of influence and impact on the environment in which we exist. What is far more exciting is the chemistry of many Exceptional individuals within a culture that values Achievement/ Merit. Fourth Century BC Athens was such a place, and it is not by any accident that twenty five hundred years later we are still discussing their philosophy of humanity and its place in the cosmos; for these truth are universal.

So it is important to ignore the present obsession with mediocrity and the knee jerk reaction to label anything or anyone as "privileged". Individuals like Carol are Exceptional and through hard work possess the " Earned Recognition and Distinction" which rightly belongs to them. Carol's self discipline, direction and dedication requires much personal sacrifice; not of course for everyone. Yet, the results such disciplines create benefited not only Carol, but all of the individuals that she interacts with.

One of the primary objectives of my book is to restore the luster to those who have strived, sacrificed and, through merit have gone beyond the norm to lift themselves up to a place, not of privilege, but of achievement that is worthy of distinction.

Being Exceptional and believing in a Culture of Exceptionalism is not a symbol of classism or oppression, but of the special opportunity and freedom for the human spirit to empower the creative impetus of our DNA to fulfill its destiny.

CLARITY

CLARITY IS THE SINGLE MOST IMPORTANT INDICATOR of a critical mind that not only survives but actually thrives in the noisy panic of our present over-plugged into society. While many wax philosophically about Critical Thinking skills and the ability to multi-task in the midst of a world where there are too many shiny distractions, unnecessary disruptions and constant distortions of fact, few actually apply these skills with any great level of effective proficiency.

It's curious that many healthy octogenarians with whom I interact have far better recall and clarity than most of the Millennials I know. All of these eighty plus year old friends are educated, filled with life experience and all have some very specific life purpose. Yet, what distinguishes them from my Millennials is their ability to know what shiny distracting objects are never to be invested one moment or ounce of energy into their consideration. This is the single most valuable skill in our hyper-active, information obsessed lives.

In present times the individual does not possess the luxury of culling through all of the rocks to find the diamond. This level of Self-Aware Perception saves and preserves the most valued capital, of which there is only a finite amount; time. This Perception (and the Clarity that it externally manifests) brings into focus so many of the Seven Exceptional Alpha Attributes. It paints a big picture with a long-term, that critically scrutinizes all of the small insignificant pleasures, quickly putting them into their proper perspective.

This Clarity strengthens a long list of Selfhood Talents which form all of the cornerstones of our Emotional Intelligence. Sad to say, but I have met many super intellectual people who lack this Emotional Intelligence and not one of them, despite all their divine gifts, ever amount to anything of significance. Just like the Parable of the Sower and the Seeds, their talents were squandered by the complexity of life; for once you are lost, it is even more difficult to find your way back.

Among the individuals that I have worked with, those who have not put it all together by thirty years old, experience a most difficult life which never reaches the full fruition of their potential. This has perplexed me for many years. I often think of making custard with my grandmother. There is a simple list of ingredients but a very specific method of cooking. One incorrect step changes the results and there is no method to right the process once it has been impaired. The same holds true for Emotional Intelligence. Too many negative experiences creates a kind of tangling of their internal wiring. Even with the best help that I could apply our steps back to the light were all short term and unsustainable. Individual's cannot build an Exceptional Tower of Achievement, if the foundation is riddled with holes.

BIG PICTURE VISION
LIFE PURPOSE   FORWARD ROADMAP

My most successful student is Exceptional in all dimensions of Self and as I pondered the Seven Alpha Attributes, he was the template.

One of the middle children of eight siblings, his working class family was renowned for their scholar athlete reputation. My first impression of this well scrubbed, Howdy Doody- hair parted to the side young man was of the 1950's; someone kind of nerd-like. Yet his gleaming smile, confident gate and firm handshake told me that I had just met someone very special; Exceptional.

From our first conversation, he exhibited, even at that young age all the smells and bells of someone who had what it took and was going to hit that ball out of the park. He knew who he was, knew what he wanted, knew what it would take to get there and was committed to investing the time and resources to make it happen. This type of Big Picture Vision is rare in people of his age. One of the attributes that formed the framework to guide him was his personalized faith, which is far different from being externally religious, as Frank believed he had a Life Purpose. At such a young age, he understood what his destiny was to be and he wouldn't let any obstacle prevent him from completing its fulfillment.

In our first discussion he explicitly rolled out his Forward Roadmap and with that Howdy Doody smile, did not skip a beat to ask me, "Can you help me make this happen?" Thirty plus years later, all that was said on the first day happen like clockwork, not by luck or through my special interest connections, but through working hard to implement the plan we discussed on that first day.

Frank is an investment banker who is a general partner at one of midtown's most esteemed international trust organizations, with a who's who list of clients. He lives in the Upper East Side with his wife and five children. He exhibits an impressive array of intellectual abilities that are the fruits of his diligence. Yet the roots of that tree reside in the soil of a man who is extremely emotionally integrated.

His Self-Aware Perception fast forwards, anything shallow or temporary, as his time-demand is huge, not just for his clients, but for his family. Frank's clarity makes him Exceptional in everything that he does. Whether it's in the role of coach of his child's baseball team, Sunday School Teacher or board member for a local charity, his holistic life is the living representation of that Big Picture Vision. This centering perspective annuls all of the toxic stress of his lofty position. Yet, make no mistake, not unlike Carol mentioned earlier in the book, there is a constant vigilance at work against anything that is unconscious or impulsive; for only through self directed behavior can anyone become Exceptional.

LISTEN — LEARN — IMPROVE

There would appear to be three easy things to do, but most people have trouble staying on track with all three simultaneously.

Some people just love to hear themselves talk and even when they engage in a conversation with you, they are hearing what they want but are not listening to everything. The older I get, the more my appreciation increases for just how essential the Art of Listening is to the process of learning and improving yourself.

It is a major problem of our times. I cannot tell you how many presentations that I've made and it is more than obvious that while people are physically present in the room, they are mentally checked out to some place far away. This past summer as I made a presentation that took me more than a month to put together, somewhere at about the fifteen minute mark the Scandinavian Crew all started taking out their iPhones and scrolling while I was speaking. To an "Old School" guy like myself, the list of negative connotations would fill this page. Respecting my host, at her family business, I did not call them out, but in any other arena there would be a strong dose of verbal castor oil harshly administered; at this late stage of my life, I do not reward anyone's bad behavior. To add insult to injury one of their team asked some pseudo- intellectual question which made it abundantly obvious that he was neither multi-tasking nor listening, but was in his own disrespectful personal Idaho. In my after meeting with my partner, I let her know that under no circumstances at even triple the price, would I work with these people, for their personal culture was not congruent with my high standards.

There is no doubt in my mind that many of you can identify with such a situation. The obsessive compulsion with being Plugged In to the latest flashes of shiny things on our cell phones have made people, who are limited in the perceptive abilities to begin with, even more socially and cognitively impaired. Few people I meet actually master the discretion of using this remarkable piece of technology well, as a vehicle to improve themselves. Such an abundance of useless images/ noise to bring meaning to a so many empty lives. This endorphin sparked addiction clouds Self Awareness in a thick fog of Self-Validation. Instead of capturing a "Eureka Moment", they are transfixed with their Self-Reflection in that small screen in the palm of their hand...how pathetic!

The ancient philosopher said it best, "How can you see the bottom of the pond, when you are always stirring its muddy waters?" The consistent common attributes of all Exceptional people, are their focus on Deep Listening, fascination with Learning New Things and a burning passion for Continuous Improvement. I can forgive the Scandinavian Crews disrespect, but I cannot pardon the impact their dysfunctional behavior had on the other people in the room, who were Listening, Learning and Improving themselves.

COSMOPOLITAN — RELEVANT — VERSATILE

In the hyper bolt of surging energy which is our globally shrinking and always connected world community, Clarity requires some automatic presuppositions. Being provincial, narrow minded, dogmatic or irrational exhibitions of judgment where lines are drawn in the sand greatly lessen your fluid effectiveness in our current world.

Erudite, cosmopolitan, relevant and versatile behaviors puts you in the heart of all worthy things and opens your eyes to all of the opportunities that await your golden touch to make them part of your Big Picture Vision. Sorry to say, its not a new recipe, for in the first century Roman Empire, all of the effective Thought Leaders of the times possessed the personal attributes that I previously mentioned. No better examples can I offer than Saint Peter and Paul who were both rural kinds of guys, whom through their scholarship and wits became two of the most Exceptional, Significant individuals of all times.

This open mental flexibility produces sparkling Clarity, as the individual is like this super dry sponge, quickly absorbing an eclectic cocktail of a diverse of experiences. The ability for the individual to comfortably transverse multiple time zones, cultures, locations and mindsets, is yet another Exceptional Beta Behavior.

My staff would marvel as we touched down in Bahrain, to see me transform into the local operating style, as I haggled with the taxi driver, where such things are the norm. Having traveled so much for business, I followed the advice of a well known Boston politician who remarked "all politics are local". The same holds true for culture, as people become comfortable with what they know. Having grown up in an ethnic subculture, from my earliest memory being flexible was a normal part of life, resulting in a love for the cultures of other people. I immersed myself in their history, language and traditions from a young age, with deep respect for anyone that had pride in their roots. Long before people spoke of Globalism, this inclusive philosophy followed my personal belief that all people were basically good and that you had to meet them where they are comfortable.

Fifty years later, having circled the globe many times, I delight at the diversity of the customers that I encounter each day. There is such Instant Magic, the moment you speak to them in their native language, as you can feel all barriers melt right before your eyes; for you have demonstrated your sincerity to meet them where they live. English speakers have become insulated as our language is the Global Lingua Franca, but should take a lesson from Saint Peter and Paul, who were exceptional polyglots. Clarity requires a point of reference that is not egocentric, but centered on the other individual's requirements and their point of reference. To be effective you must always follow this advice..... It is Never About Me- It is Always About the Other Person.

ACCURACY

Accuracy

THIS IS ANOTHER HUGE CHALLENGE IN OUR SOCIETY but with each passing year the bar moves lower and lower. Often people tell me to just relax and don't sweat the small stuff; things always find a way of sorting themselves out. Worse, is the entire Hukuna Matata (from the Lion King movie) Crew who are even more chilled out and have no worries at all, drifting through life like a leaf being blown in the wind. At the opposite end are the people so maxed out, that even their best intentions results in well over fifty percent of the stuff they do being sloppy and incorrect. What makes this worse is that they are well aware that their work is inferior and substandard but will be quick to tell you their intentions are so sincere so that should count for a lot. Effort matters ?!

As much as in my heart of hearts I love sincere people, my head follows a simple prescription; 1 + 2 + 3 + 4 = 10. Yes, ten, not nine and a half or nine and three quarters. It has to be ten. The thing that these people just don't get, so many people in other places far across the globe who are our competitors living their entire lives always seeking to give you a ten; every time!

The sad fact, in this harsh, rough and tumble world in which we live, the people that tell you to "not sweat the small stuff" are foolish as that one missing detail will come back and bite you with lethal ferocity. On a higher level of thinking as strategists, doing it correctly the first time conserves time and resources but also builds a reputation of Excellence that increases your influential impact on an ever widening circle.

As I construct this new multi-million dollar product, it is not the professionals around the corner that I've chosen to partner with, but people six thousand miles away. Yes, it is their love of Accuracy but also their understanding that it takes a process of Precision to consistently produce that type of quality. Their objective is always 10, …not 9 ½ …or 9 ¾ ; but 10. What I love even more about them is that their Precision is not some stiff apparatchik rote but a clarity of expression which is both creative and precise at the same time. Their aspirational and optimistic energy captures the zest for life that I want my product to bring into the world.

Maybe it's the Affluenza and the comfort of our society in America but with the exception of only a very small group of "High Flying Millennials" I find most people as dull as a forty watt yellow light bulb, requiring repeating the same instruction several times and then checking their work at least three more times when it is completed. Nevertheless patience comes with being an elder, I advise, assist and encourage, still it is most disconcerting that I must travel six thousand miles to find people who actually appreciate this concept.

ANALYTICAL AWARENESS
FIND — KNOW ALL THE DOTS

You would think with a process that is as simple as Hansel and Gretel's trail of breadcrumbs everyone could tune into their intuition and figure out how and where all of the dots are located. However in today's highly distracted world, many people have shut that switch off a long time ago and in fact forget all the dots; they don't even know where the switch is located anymore.

I meet many people who have "Checked Out" from the sensory experience they are interacting within. It is acculturated behavior that is mystifying to an old school person like myself. My greatest revelation was in observing people walking around this breathtakingly beautiful pond on an early August morning, as the cool air mingles with the warming sunshine, birds were singing as the trees canopy your every footstep. It was like being in the most majestic of places that was not built with human hands. While I'm having some near out of body spiritual experience, absorbing the wonder of the moment, I see others with two plugs in their ears, enabling some obviously loud music to blast through their head.

I'm not judging their choice of music but I am questioning why anyone who could be experiencing such an awesome environment feels compelled to have some type of distraction from what they have come to believe, is a medium of entertainment. We have all seen these people that are just so "plugged in" and always removing themselves from the here and now. Before you judge me harshly, let me demonstrate what these two different mindsets produce.

One of my brightest little lightbulbs lives in the here and now all of the time, but wisely uses technology. I just adore his critical thinking skills and acute analytical awareness. He was accepted to attend college and went with some reservations. After attending one class at the local college, he called to tell me that it was not going to work out. I immediately visited him. Rather than attempting to convince him, I listened to his cause and effect calculations. We immediately went to speak with an administrator and turned that ship around. Years later, this very well-to-do businessman, who knew where his dots were to be found exalts in my confidence in him…Actually, it was easy, for he discovered what he wanted by experiencing what he didn't want. Conversely, I have had several other students who lived in that world of 24/7 distraction, where this process took one or even two years of college to figure out. It took a lots of worry, poor grades and most regrettably considerable student debt to arrive at the same point as my Bright Little Lightbulb after a one hour and half class. His Exceptional judgement comes from the precise manner in how he analyzes everything. Having the personal confidence to believe in what he intuitively feels gives him a most valuable competitive advantage, for he is constantly aware of his surroundings.

EXACTING PRECISION
CONNECT ALL THE DOTS

What makes my Little Lightbulb so bright is not just his ability to embrace his strong analytical skills but the Tenacity to put the energy into doing whatever it takes to connect all of the dots ; for success, in the final analysis, is 99% perspiration. This is one to the great failures of my very well-intentioned "helicopter parent" generation, we love them so much that we have never allowed our children to develop the thick resilient skin to push back hard at the harshly toxic society that exists today. My Little Lightbulb's parents suffered no such affliction, and from an early age it was spoonfuls of Yankee castor oil direction that molded his mind into this very sensitive but remarkably strong willed individual.

His is a strictly an internal process, that is deeply introspective. It is not manifested in hyper-aggressive speech or behavior, but a gentle strength which if you are attuned, allows to feel his energy the moment that you meet him. In today's world, it is not enough to know what you want out of life but you must back it up with sincere passion. This type of confidence is discouraged by those who attempt to diminish the value of personal merit; as it quickly distinguishes the milk from the cream. In our society of entitlement people such as the my Little Lightbulb experience countless daily images that challenge their lifestyle philosophy. Challenges quickly deflated, like a balloon to pricked by a large hat pin; as merit is a cumulative process, whose beneficial results are building all the time.

A more dramatic tale, is one of my students who hailed from Iowa, from a place that had more hogs than people. His dream was to become an Ivy League Professor. Where he was born was so remote, that it was the location that after you arrived at "No-Where" you still had to drive another half an hour get to his home town. This is the bucolic place that this little boy with big dreams grew up. His simple rural life had all the wonderful individuals and institutions that have shaped some of the best people that we have ever produced in this country.

The success ingredients were similar to many other Exceptional people mentioned in this book, hard working family, lots of direction/ discipline and an astounding Aspirational Perspective on Life. Just like my Little Lightbulb, the process was completely self contained. From crawling, to baby steps, to walking, to running and then sprinting at full throttle, he advanced out of that hamlet, to the county and on to statewide and national to now at a global level of success. His overwhelming success factor was developing a specific recipe and with Exacting Precision executing it flawlessly ten thousand times. He proves to me that it is not always the most gifted that arrive at those places of distinction but the most determined who value Accuracy and leave no dot unturned.

METICULOUS EXECUTION
ORGANIZE ALL THE DOTS

So this process of creating Exceptional Accuracy is a three legged milk stool. It is not enough to possess the awareness of all the dots and recipe to connect them for if you truly want to be Exceptional you must be constantly be creatively seeking to improve the quality of all the dots and the process of making them work better.

It is the basis story of civilization's advancement. Better Quality, Quicker Results, Less Expense with an easier entry point and learning curve that creates greater opportunity for everyone is the reoccurring tale of Human Achievement. In our world of greater and greater connectivity any image to conveys that paradigm in a split second is creative gold and the next billion dollar product.

As I developed our Talent Types System, the single-minded objective was to improve the quality of life through creating an instrument that would bring improved opportunity to a larger number of people. What were the necessary dots to achieve this? How could these dots be utilized best in the most user friendly process? How much up front "sweat equity" would be necessary to keep the cost model down so the entry price would be half of our competitors, therefore allowing more people access to its benefits? This greater opportunity factor was, personally, very important to me. In essence, it was a tale of listening to what the dots were telling us.

In looking at the existing assessment test, that has dominated the market for years. I found it was unnecessarily lengthy and complex. There were too many dots!

Re-engineering the dots required research and testing to see if fewer dots in the assessment model produced equally valid results. Once we discovered fewer dots worked, then we carefully crafted a precise process that would turn out a consistently excellent product. Finally, through having a simpler model with less dots we produced a technical platform that was far easier to use and more rapid in delivering even more reliable results.

Our Talent Types test requires seventy percent less testing time and delivered more accurate, user friendly information that provided the client with a competitive advantage in which to make decisions more speedily than non users. With an operating model that was better and quicker, we could offer our users a price that was fifty percent less than the prevailing market rate. Our persistence and patience to work out a Precise Process created an outstanding product. Our Talent Type Best Quality story is one of meticulous execution; finding, knowing, connecting and organizing all of the dots into a new matrix which becomes our Masterpiece Creation.

EXCELLENCE

Excellence may very well be one of the most overused words in our everyday lexicon, but for all the jibber-jabber; do most people produce excellent work every day? If you talk to the Learning and Training Specialists at the Fortune 100 Corporations, (after they roll their eyes at your naïveté and professionally hold it all together as not to present a poor first impression with you); they look you dead in the eye and say No. In fact, the billions of dollars each year expended, support their unequivocal answer.

So, is excellence a natural state of mind? Don't all people want to create a masterpiece in everything that they do? Are people, by their nature not diligent but more likely to take the easy way out all the time? Is the way we view our own personal excellence tied to the manner in which we see our own self-image? Certainly a lot of questions, and with time, I have an answer for each one.

I imagine back in prehistoric times, that excellence in the quality of what you did was a primary determination of your ability to live or die. Not to get all Darwinian, but there was a pecking order within the species, the smart strong ones ascended and let's just say that the descendants of the others, the Neanderthals were the Edsels of the species and had a very short shelf life. Our species, in the subsequent experience of hundreds of generations developed a DNA that was formulated for both excellence and success. Yes, Excellence is a natural state of mind and along with that, every individual possesses a fundamental impetus to be a source of creation and regeneration. These wonderful qualities are hardwired in our DNA and are automatically accessed through our intuition.

The great short circuit of this remarkable electrical system starts with our life of Affluenza and a liberal philosophy that discourages merit and fosters entitlement. These two factors are the greatest impediment to excellence in our nation today. To those of you who disagree, I invite you to research the ever growing amount of dollars invested into training people "things" that only a generation ago were a natural outcropping of Common Sense.

"Remind" is the key learning word that best describes how managers are instructed in their training on how to effectively motivate their teams. The best performing team I have observed, has a manager who, every day, reminds the team of the basic objectives and metrics that they are seeking to achieve. To further verify this, I experimented and had that manager leave out several of the score card metrics. Time after time and location after location those omitted metrics fell instantly, only to be restored after they were reinserted as part of the daily pep rally script. The entire phenomenon reveals something about our present state of mind.

SUPERIOR QUALITY

The good, better and best ascendency has a direct link to the manner in which the individual views their self image. I was raised in a discriminated ethnic subgroup who over came a plethora of unfairness by being the best all of the time. It was our shield and sword when remarks about our inferiority were thrust upon us. The merit of our earned achievement told the harsh outside world; sorry, even by your rules, 1 + 1 does not equal 3. This Beta Behavior is the heart and soul of being Exceptionally Excellent.

Back in the early 1970's an immigrant family opened a pizza place in a small town. Their operating model was simple; to create the best consistent product. They believed that they were only one bad pizza away from going out of business. If the green peppers on their pizza cost $25 per case in season and $100 per case out of season, they absorbed the cost and never deviated from the quality. Each pizza was a personal representation of who they were and what they believed. Their Superior Quality food, in a place where at that time there were no other pizza places fueled surging interest and business. One by one, they opened more restaurants and brought additional family members to America to work and then eventually start their own businesses. Nearly fifty years later, this tribe of extended families have a state-wide and long list of locations. During that time, they have gone toe-to-toe with national chain pizza restaurants and new local competitors, but their philosophy and ability to market themselves strategically have consistently put all of their competition out of business.

They are Exceptional in having discovered a specific success recipe whose cornerstone of Superior Quality and Value never wavered from that high standard. Their competitors inability to consistently satisfy their standard of Superior Quality and Value, which had become the acculturated expectation of their local customer base, provided them with a Loyalty Culture that no one could break. That Loyalty Culture is founded on their belief that each one of their pizzas are a Signature Experience.

FLAWLESS EXECUTION

The quality of the Signature Experience is to be unique while at the same time creating an exciting expectation that stimulates the customer with anticipation. This requires expertise and self-discipline to flawlessly, but more importantly, creatively execute every single time. Not an easy task, for it requires managing a lot of factors that are within your control, and the more daunting external conditions that your expertise must accommodate to achieve that level of Superior Quality.

A useful analogy that I might offer is of one of my students, who was an excellent baseball pitcher. He was exceptional in the execution of his craft; a real star.

From the outside you would believe that it was simply his natural talent, but once you stripped off all of the bravado and ego; a more complete picture emerged.

I remember an archbishop telling me, " excellent priests were not educated at the seminary, but formed by their families." Such is the story of Flawless Execution. Our pitcher came from a baseball dynasty of players. Generations of superb athletes who formed a sports family culture. So from the earliest age, drop by drop, the excellence of his craft was based upon layers and layers of experiences that molded and then polished his skills. Along with that was a unbelievable amount of training and practice time. The old adage that "practice makes perfect" is completely true. If you want to hit that ball out of the park in every game you must expend tenfold the time and resources to back it up. There are no free lunches.

This investment in yourself yields excellent results which can only improve the more you follow your Success Path Recipe. What adds to the complexity is the mindset that you possess. Being compulsive, overbearing, arrogant or elitist about your flawless performance, diminishes the Signature Experience you bring to others. All of the Exceptional people I meet are always low keyed and humble about their talent. The vast majority of them have a concept that it is a gift that as easily as it was given, could be even more quickly gone. Through their hard work they know the amount of determination it takes to stay at that Exceptional Level.

PRIDE OF AUTHORSHIP

Just like all the " Signature Pizzas" there is a strong Pride of Authorship in creating Exceptional Excellence. I've seen this "Signature Authorship" over and over again with anyone who takes pride in their work. This is another one of the building blocks in the Excellence Pyramid. It is what make something good into something that is great.

I had a student who was an orphan; in fact he did not even know his father. This cloud was something that I spent considerable time trying to dispel the depressive tone it lent to his life. Great people prevail over adversity and the hottest fires produce the best steel. So with years of encouragement, this loss became a big plus to him. Paul was a strong student with excellent grades and big dreams, but due to his circumstances was a social pariah. I told him that "once he went to college, away from the unfair judgement of his little Peyton Place Town; his rose would come into full bloom. This promise brought him much hope and spurred him onward.

After three months of being in college, he came home for the Holidays and his transformation into a swan was breathtaking. All of the pain and sorrow were gone. There he stood with a new leather jacket and a confident smile; our little rocket had left the Launch pad. His academic career in college was stellar as Paul had found that his meritorious achievements told the outside world his true story.

He graduated college and accepted an entry level position. The quality of his work ethic and the Signature Experience he created for his customers quickly advanced him upward. In the space of three years, he had several promotions and had nearly doubled his entry salary. Yet, life throws all of us a curve ball and the Great Recession came. His entire department was disbanded and he was unemployed. My guidance was clear, keep paddling forward, as only good things would come to an individual who produces such excellent quality as he did.

He accepted a service position that paid the bills. While at that position, a recruiter called him after viewing his profile on line. After some telephone interviews, they flew him to California where once again he gave them a Signature Experience Interview. This was further supported by his references, which praised his exceptional work performance. An offer was extended that was almost three times his current service position salary. In a month's time he was clear across the country living the dream he told me about the first day we had met.

So what made him such a "Stand Out"? It was his Exceptional Excellence in who he was as a person and in how he manifested it every day by his actions. More than a fairy tale, this is a true life story of the possibilities that exist for an individual who would invest in themselves and make a commitment to take that extra step. Paul inspires me to dream that all things are possible to those who believe in divine energy that strengthens them to believe in themselves. There is still an American Dream for those who will have the vision and hard core determination to defy the odds and audaciously reached for.

LEGACY IMPACT

This is the Super Bowl in the Art of Exceptional Excellence, as the individuals who perfects this level of performance has the added transcendent dimension of knowing that their actions will have an impact far beyond the present. I have met certain gifted individuals in the Fall and Winter Seasons of their life: high performing executives and their teams, well-respected statesmen, professional sports teams and beloved public figures, who possess a keen awareness that their talent is extraordinary and will become the gold standard for many years to come. Those individuals who have the ability to chronicle their story, write their own history and craft an image that remains long after they are gone. The best measure of our life is to do something that will outlast us. Another side of the Creation Gene is the desire for some type of immortality. Pharaohs built pyramids, others endowed buildings and institutions inscribed with their name; for to be Exceptional is to be remembered.

I had a long time friend, advisor and political confidant who every Saturday at 5:00 PM I would meet at his jewelry store. At the heart of our deep friendship was our altruistic intentions, which sparked a very long list of town and community projects. We were not interested in getting our names on some old dusty placards, but quietly accomplishing improvements that would have a significant impact on the future of the community. Our efforts were always quite secretive as to not garner attention, which would hamper our effectiveness and diminish the quality of our objectives.

Our primary focus was to bring additional arts and educational opportunities to our little town. One of the wonderful things about living in a small fish bowl, is that everything is a microcosm of life, and due to the small size, you could readily observe the positive impact of your initiatives more rapidly.

Our most ambitious project was to create additional educational opportunities; outside tutoring, S.A.T. Prep, college advising, and massive financial aid incentives, along with a social support system.

Our ambitious project was put into place, piece by piece, like a complex jigsaw puzzle. The most important factor was to shoot for the stars, as we knew the higher we attempted to reach, the greater the future impact would be. Of course we had our critics, those that called us elites, politically motivated and a host of other nonsensical utterances that small minds in small towns enjoy generating maliciously. Only once did someone actually openly comment and tell me that our ideas were "uppity". My response was simple, "My time, my money and my business." There was dissent as our students were not going to the local community college or the state schools but to private universities throughout the nation. Once Talent is stretched, it can never go back to the size and shape it was before. Undeterred, years and decades later we kept going.

Twenty years later, our cohort of students are professionals who work on a global level. The large corporations value their exceptional social skills that were formed by living in a small rural town where there are no separations or categories. We are a small community of neighbors. Their client friendly, positive attitudes are the lingua franca of customer relations; the gold standard that corporations just love. As I scroll through my Linked-In contacts and read a who's who of corporations where they have all advanced to become both significant and most prosperous, all I can do is smile. My friend has long passed on to his reward, but I know he too is smiling from above as our most lasting legacy impact was to produce an entire generation of successful individuals.

The most Exceptional thing that you can do with your life is to create something that will outlast you long after you're gone….Our Love changed the course of lives and the future.

CONSISTENT

I RECENTLY WAS WATCHING THE WHITE HOUSE CORRESPONDENTS DINNER which is a gathering of media glitterati and moguls to celebrate themselves. I was transfixed on how you could have so many inauthentic, insincere and completely useless people gathered in one room. In one location you have the very worst elements of American Culture, of which tens of millions of regular folks have voiced their disapproval, by their vote for a presidential candidate that has so openly exposed the hypocrisy of their place in American Society.

How anyone of substance could even break bread with these parasites, astounds me; for there is a paradigm shift underway in our society as the gap between these people and regular Americans grows ever wider. A bumper sticker that I saw the other day summarizes this best, " I Don't Trust The Mainstream Media".

What's significant here, is to be Exceptional is to be Trusted as a consistent and dependable resource partner. Americans have little if no trust in a list of critical institutions, as each one has failed them repeatedly; #1 Politicians and #2 the Media. So as this collection of fools celebrate themselves in the glow of the Beltway, the very ground they are standing on is moving in the other direction. One thing this election cycle has revealed is that there is a growing anger that the elite can no long satiate with Bread and Circus. The horses are all out of the barn and running to who knows where; seismic change is coming.

These dynamics even ripple to a small town like ours that is at the end of the rail line. As I speak to persons after person, there is a consistent theme;

let's throw the bums out. Having been a publicly elected official for almost thirty years, I reflect on some of the Exceptional public figures with whom I have worked. What Alpha Attributes made them so beloved? In our Live Free or Die State, it is all a matter of Integrity and having the Common Touch. These two factors create a relational bond with a wide constituency. If you are both highly educated and affluent but only focus on your humility; the people will love you even more. This simple wisdom eludes the glitterati in places like NYC, Beverly Hills and the Beltway; where authentic honesty is a most endangered trait.

STRONG CHARACTER
INTEGRITY

The American public is a most forgiving lot and will cut you some slack for just about anything. The one exception is if they catch you in a lie. This breach of character is a nonstarter and fatal to any future attempts to inspire the public trust. It's not a matter of any indiscretion already committed, but most people do not have the energy to worry about what dishonest thing you're going to do next.

Yet, lying has become a big part of all too many people's lifestyle. Some tell me its situational and make it easier to deal with a conflict; while others confidently profess its all part of the power and influence game.

The impact is a cancer to relationships and a calculated risk, for once discovered, the damage is done; usually permanently. When I think about the people that I most admire and why; it was centered on their Integrity.

Having served on a state-wide position as treasurer, at the beginning of my tenure I sought out the best auditors. This position was most visible with a high public exposure profile. This condition having no impact upon me, as I believe that if you always do the right thing and act with the best of your abilities; no one can harm you… or so I thought!

Having served in my position for fifteen years, a situation arose that required me to challenge the establishment "elites", as their actions were adverse to our best practice standards. Their power-politics approach was to first attack me, then to attempt to discredit me and finally to remove me. They attempted to create a justification for their actions and manufacture a story that they could spin. So their counsel brutally browbeat a list of our partner resources in order to subvert the facts.

All of them stood tall but none taller than my auditor who drew a line in the sand that they could not cross. The powerful opposition employed other means of leverage that all proved to be most ineffective. Our actions supported the professional standards of the best practices that were part and parcel of our auditor-client agreement. What was there to discuss? The powerful have such difficulty when they can't get their way!

This clarity confounded our adversaries, as truth possesses a certain universal power that speaks for itself. Like a person in a poker game who held a bad hand of cards, they folded and went away licking their wounds. The unwavering consistency of my auditor was exceptional, in light of the pressure that was placed upon him to compromise his personal beliefs. In that moment of crisis, he was the ultimate Alpha Leader.

VALUES PEOPLE RELATIONSHIPS

Another trusted political advisor who has been a constant thorn in the side of the establishment elites, earned her considerable leverage through her embrace of people. She is the consummate laborer in the political arena. Many town officials, legislators and national candidates owe their victories to her vast relational network.

While the "elites" are hypnotically drawn to power like a moth to a bright flame, she just likes to help others and has built a state, if not national reputation, one constituent at a time. Hers is not a fair weather friendship but true blue, as she invests herself into everything with such sincerity and an amazing, tireless Yankee work ethic.

Like the unsinkable Molly Brown, her defeats are brief, but even in the face of a loss; she dusts herself off to keep on going. Her bright optimism is further enhanced but her memory of thousands of names and facts. This gift of spontaneous recall makes her a formidable opponent, as anyone in the loyal opposition would be first to tell you. Even more than the official state party organization, her state-wide team shoulders tremendous gravitas with which to influence a situation. It further attests to the power of people over money, as exampled by her organization which runs on a decimal fraction of the state party's operating budget. Her leadership, effusive personality and brilliant strategic mind quickly closes the funding gap, which no doubt keeps the establishment elites up at night.

In the midst of my political crisis, she was a champion and helped develop our strategy to be ten steps ahead of our ferocious, untamed adversaries. Every attempt they mustered was a day late and a dollar short, as we had already counted all of the noses of the horses on our team; their commitments resting safely in our pocket.

More than the thrust and the parry of this childish battle, the legislation that she has partnered and passed has improved the lives of Granite Staters. It is her belief in people and the value of true blue and honest relationship that makes her exceptional.

KEEPS WORD
DEPENDABLE

This is another beta behavior that is esteemed by everyone. Trusted individuals are dependable; the cornerstone of your Loyalty Culture. Each day, in the context of the toxic society we all must audaciously encounter, the orbits of Loyal Partners form a force field of strength. How can anyone create consistent Signature Experiences if their stable of operation is filled with mares of questionable integrity? The Scripture says, "Let your Yeas be Yeas and your Nays be Nays". If your house is not built upon this solid footing, you are wasting valuable time/energy on people unnecessary in your life. Not to sound cold or calculating but the fact is that if you have people in your life who are inconsistent or undependable, they are a distraction and should be placed on your back burner. We all have earned the luxury of surrounding ourselves with quality people who love you as much as you love them. Anything short of that is time wasted, and in this New Century…Time is the Ultimate Currency.

I know through much personal pain that I would gladly choose silent piece of mind over any flashy fake smile. Flash people come and go, in and out of your life. They remind me of the bright leaves on an oak tree, that cycle from green, to yellow, then crimson and finally muddy brown. Yet my old gnarled oak tree is not as exciting but its deep roots brings shade to my home in the Summer and shields it from the harsh Winter winds. I am most thankful for such a good friend. Yes, consistent people may not be as exciting or as pretty as the bright leaves, but they are dependable for they keep their word to stand by us; always giving their very best portion.

As much as the world of politics is not a place for the faint of heart, the world of church politics casts even greater shadows of duplicity. In the dangerous cross winds of all too many personal agendas, how do you build dependable Loyalty Partners? Either by finding a pious elder who you can trust or by carefully selecting some talented young person who your intuition tells you, is worthy of your trust. I prefer the second choice, as this lump of gifted earth can be crafted, then filled with your experienced wisdom. Out of all my many novitiates, there is one who stands head and shoulders above all of the rest.

Granted, he has an excellent singing voice, gives a fantastic homily, works well with all of the youth groups but so do the majority of all the seminarian that I have mentored. Their outward behavior displays all the perfected skills that this most demanding profession expects. What makes Christos so special, is the quality of his heart. He is my Go-To-Guy, even though he comes from halfway across the planet; just like the old Yankee farmer whose handshake is as good as a signed agreement his word is his bond. In the dozen years that I have known him he has never once disappointed me. Just like my auditor and political strategists, he possesses all of those Empathic Qualities that has taken them years to develop, but what makes him uniquely exceptional is that he is twenty five years younger than both of them. I often joke with him that he possesses wisdom far beyond his Millennial years.

He does not have that charismatic instant dazzle that sweeps you off your feet, like the bright oak leaf. What he has is far better, for just like the oak tree, he is a "Keeper". Early in his career many were skeptical about him and told me that he lacked humility, as his talent and the precision with which he executed them were far beyond his young years. His gifts made others, especially those that lacked passion for their ministry, extremely uncomfortable. I in turn modeled to him the value of loyalty, using my reputation along with my family's dynastic clerical pedigree to be a formidable champion advocate. My fatherly protection provided him time to mature and build his sterling reputation. I told him, " Sometimes it takes others much longer to figure out what our strong intuition absorbs the first time, instantly." The witness my Loyalty Partnership demonstrates, inspires him to follow my lead and develop these type of consistent trusting relationships. ... that in today's world are truly Exceptional.

CONFIDENT

As I assessed this Alpha Attribute and attempted to define it, after much deliberation, I chose the word Confident. Yet, this is not some kind of ego adventure Confidence like Indiana Jones in "The Raiders of the Lost Ark." There is no bravado, puffed up minds and bodies, certain indicators of a hyperaggressive character. This Confidence is subtle and sure. The more Exceptional the individual, the more modulated is their low key manner. Theirs's is a Confidence of substance not style.

While all too many in our society have this flashy/shallow Confidence that's borne out of pure vanity, the Exceptional individual's Confidence is grounded in their expertise knowledge. They are all very well aware of their giftedness, to various degrees, but the greater they are, the more self-effacing and humble I found these individuals. They have no problem laughing at themselves or others pointing out the more than usually eccentric behavior. In fact many of them wear their eccentricity like a badge of honor, as their counter-culture behavior empowers them against the toxic mainstream culture, that they have demystified, rendering it as benign, with a formidable social iconoclasm that mocks its insincere actions.

Each one of these people has their own specific process of Individualization; no two are completely alike. This emphasizes that we all do have our own unique personal story to bring into the world. We all are a miracle of life, but it is the life choices and the philosophy which we embrace that allows those gifts to rise and blossom one hundred fold or die as they are choked by the weeds of a harsh world.

The other character of this Confidence is another counter-culture feature; loving gentleness. These are very secure people who are filled with so much love and never refrain from expressing that to the people who surround them. Their hopeful brightness is infectious, as this Good Karma energy captures your attention. I honestly had to debate whether Confident or Hopeful were the correct words to use in defining this Alpha Attribute. Hopeful is more of an emotional quality, while Confident possesses a strong rooting in our intellect. Make no mistake these Exceptional, Confidently Hopeful individuals are as bright as a light bulb.

OPTIMISTIC — GRATEFUL — ENCOURAGING

All three of the individuals that I will describe in this chapter have an effusive charismatic quality that captures your attention from the moment that you meet them. It is a not simply a Signature Experience, but more like a WOW Moment, as they are not Exceptional in one specific area; everything they do has a much larger than life quality. They all possess a fascinating balance of intellectual energy with deep empathic concern, not for the sake of achievement but for the people with whom they partner in the process of making things happen. Their people/ soft skills only add to their effectiveness as those with whom they partner are infused with a burst of their enthusiastic energy, to take risks, reach higher and dream about the stars. All three individuals are religious, not superficially but as seekers of a spiritual fulfillment which is never publicly displayed but seeking quietly meditative fulfillment. It's my theory that they require that type of spiritual centering due the quantum intellectual abilities with which they are endowed. Their minds never shut off and even process solutions while they're sleeping; of which all three only do four hours each night. These three are the most Exceptional people I know!

If you could capture all his personal brand of sunshine in a bottle; you would only have captured a small portion of this confidently, positive man. He is the template which I use in describing this positive, hopeful and bright Confidence that all Exceptional individuals possess. His optimism is not saccharine like a cup of overly sweetened coffee but low keyed, with a very uplifting grace that pervades every interaction. Yet, he is no shrinking violet, as he has thrusted himself into the midst of some of the hottest debates that I have seen in the public arena over the last twenty five years.

Even in the midst of some horrific political battles, where he was bombarded daily by the media with statements of complete untruth, he remained resolute. Never does he waffle to soften their rhetoric. His coolness under fire and ability to see the silver lining is the type of optimistic confidence that only comes by having a very solid unified philosophy of life. His fierce and audacious intellect is tempered by a strong sense of grateful appreciation of having risen from working class poverty to a place of national prominence.

The center lynchpin that is his life compass, is to remember every day where he started and his obligation to share his journey, and in doing so creating many other stars into a constellation of light. I have called upon him, on many occasions, for direction in times of indecision and even to intervene in moments of political crisis. Risking his own talent, time and treasure, he has been my champion leader and ardent foil in defeating many political foes. Such sure footed friends are few and far between. I often joke with him, "when I grow up, I want to be just like you." Even his most acidulous opponents admire his gentlemanly elegance. He never loses his cool or raises his voice to intimidate or demand, but lets the course of his effective brilliance win the debate. It is most difficult for them to wage any personal attacks against him, as this bottle of sunshine's expressive fairness is a rare commodity. You know you're really special when all your of ideological opponents say, " I deeply admire Jack as a person but don't agree with what he believes."

EXPERT PROFICIENCY

Not a day passes in which I don't hear someone speaking out of their hat, posturing as if having a size 12 intellect when the shoebox unquestionable reveals theirs as a size 9. At this mid-point time of my life such banter is exhausting and lacks any purpose except to promote futility. It is delightfully refreshing when I hear, " I don't know the answer, but I can get back to you later." This simple utterance informs me that I have someone of substance in my presence, an individual who cares enough to know the correct answer, not simply for my sake, but for the enhancement of their own intellectual skills.

The Confidence that these Exceptional individuals profess exude a powerful intellectual base. There is a compensating emotional dimension that softens their intense brilliance as to always factor people and relationships as part of the complete solution. The reason these individuals are able to be so confident is simply because they know exactly what their talking about. There are never any gray areas and they have absolutely no interest in wowing or impressing anyone. The reason that their knowledge is so sound, is due to all of the constant hard work that they do, that is not immediately apparent the first time that you meet them.

This dynamic might as well be Peter's personal story. Your first impression is of a country doctor who works primarily with the rural poor. He has that country chic, kind of LL Bean rumpled look. To many city people when they first meet him, they casually place Peter into one to their stereotypical boxes; taking notice of the oyster but neglecting to find the hidden pearl. Their inflexible methodology brings an unhealthy amount of enjoyment to Peter; for his roots are urban, from an Ivy League family who have sat as professors at the most elite medical college on the planet. It is extremely unwise to make these off the cuff assumptions. Something that any experienced salesperson would tell you is that a frumpy exterior may very well be bed drape for your next stellar sale. Smart people never judge a book by its cover, as they open it and read the pages to discover the entire story.

Peter's almost invisible prodigiousness peeks out from his humorous view of observing the world. His remarkable disciplined mind, linked to how freely he gives the best portion of his energy to others, elevates him to expert proficiency in every thing that he does. Because he is in his mid-life and this lifestyle has been all he has known for many decades, he exudes this excellence as easily as the next breath that he takes.

The Exceptional Confidence of people like Peter is not anchored to their ego but is an expression of their natural aptitude. He is blessed to have learned at a young age to discover who he was, what were his gifts and then to find the best place to polish them for a lifetime. The recurring stratagem that I observe, is first, to discover your truth, then develop your success recipe and finally just keep doing it for a lifetime.

ASSERTIVE LEADERSHIP — ENERGETIC STRATEGIST

This is where the Confidence of the Exceptional truly kicks into high gear. Their uncontainable energy travels in a split second like light itself. Their great task is harnessing this beast that roars. As if it is not disciplined, it will not only consume you but destroy many the gifts bestowed. It is usually due to a loss of perspective, as arrogance compels us to a insatiable greed of resources and influence, where are no boundaries but a swirling tempest that rages and once unleashed it is so hard to put its magic back into a box. The demise whether quickly or painfully slowly is as tragic as Icarus, flying too high, only to fall like a stone into the sea.

Those with Mindfulness, having God in their life or some form of Selfless Virtue is like a cool drink of the living water quenching the flames of every unsatisfied ambition. This spiritual dimension of self is like the median markers on the highway; keeping you in the correct lane. Those simple little yellow lines, one after another, are insignificant by themselves, but when cumulatively joined form a matrix that is part of a unified life philosophy. I am most grateful for such helpful companions on my journey, who are always with me and never cease doing their jobs.

The quintessential achiever of all of my High Flying Millennials wrestles with his unrelenting, ambitious VisionQuest and yet the strong desire to live a healthy and moral life. It's not easy. On one hand, he is a superb business and political strategist, who is usually several steps ahead of everybody. On the other hand the circles of power he revolves in, have many people reminiscent of those at the White House Correspondence Dinner; those to whom the ends will always justify any type of means. The push and pull is epic, with a large cast of characters vying for his young, charismatic and physically attractive energy. They want to capture his soul, in some type of foible or folly in order to discredit, then destroy him.

In these moments of stress he calls, as I pastor directly to his well-developed faith based value system. To his great credit, he not only calls but listens to advice. From this, he is re-centered, re-focused and renewed. These mutual "Kairos Experiences" are difficult for him, as he is self-conscious of the vulnerable fabric of his humanity. Slowly, I poke through the veil, probe as my trained intuition hones-in, like a bloodhound to make my diagnosis. Great is the burden of some one young, to possess such gifts before their emotional framework can steer the car down the road and not cross over the yellow line. In time, I am assured that his collective wisdom and maturity will become excellent life companions. In twenty years, it is a certainty that his name will be a household word. The great danger resides within the interim period. I tell him to do nothing by impulse, but always through concerted consciousness, for this extra step tames the ego and builds deliberative skills… the epicenter of all good actions.

PRIORITY

This Alpha Attributes is one that is an instant litmus test; either your light switch is on and you get it or it's off, as life's opportunities are passing you by. There is wisdom in the aphorism, the Early Bird Always Catches the Worm. This does not mean just getting up early, but possessing a focused mindfulness that is alert to relationships, and values other people more than yourself. Respecting other people's time is a constant rant that anyone that has dealt with me has heard over and over again. I think it's huge!!

The Urgency and Priority that you bring to others makes an instant statement and draws an immediate picture of your character and even in how your brain is wired. Are you self-oriented, shallow and narcissistic or are you sincere, considerate and appreciative of others? Over the years I've had many words on this subject and have cut my loses with people who I liked considerably but who have repeatedly demonstrated that their poor upbringing, immaturity or Me- Me- Me- selfishness was something which they refused to work on and improve. Time is the ultimate currency and who in the raging roar of our 21st Century Life has the extra energy to waste on this kind of nonsense.

You must adopt a Zero Tolerance Policy in dealing with other people's poor behavior. I'm not saying to react unreasonably if someone does not do everything that you want, but a repeated pattern emerges, the behavior may become a toxic syndrome, of which you are the enabling party which only adds to their addiction. Yes, we do live in a time of great distraction. Yes, distraction whose prime causality is an addiction to be entertained 24/7 by getting a dopamine rush, as we grab our iPhone to see the latest new useless flash of light on the screen, which convinces us that we matter and that we're very special.

This year I will write five books and hundreds of additional pages of content. Not because I fancy myself possessed of some great gift but because I don't have an iPhone. I don't live in the World of Distraction or possess a mind that has an addiction to 20 Sec. Dopamine Rush Syndrome. Yes, I have FB and Linked-In, which connect me to a large collection of people who I love with my whole heart. I check these things and my email several times a day, and immediately respond to each inquiry, for it tells my Golden Circles that they are important to me. One cannot preach what one does not practice. Even from my lofty perch, removed from the nonsense of most people's difficult 21st Century Life, this sense of priority that I accord everyone sends a reassuring message that I value them that I "got their back". Repeatedly, I have been told, that this emotional blank check is the Sine Quo Non of my special relationship with so many people. Unafraid, I place myself before them, for in an action of unconditional acceptance and humility; both of which are a contrary to the prevailing Modus Operandi of the toxic mainstream. How can I be a great mentor, if I do not consistently show the benefits that Clarity, Precision and Urgency bring to a good life? How can I expect to mentor Exceptional Individuals unless I train them to love the Alpha Attributes that will make them strong and successful?

VALUE OF TIMELINESS
CAPITAL — OPPORTUNITY — RELATIONSHIP

As much as I adore the people in my ethnic sub-culture, on the subject of timeliness they would get a failing grade. They are not the only ones and it seems that every ethnic group have the same kind of stories. One of the most beneficial aspects of my Yankeeization is not only my understanding of time, but more importantly, of other people's time. 12:00 means 12:00. Slicing and dicing this to 12:10 or 12:15 or still worse, 12:30, is just plain rude and inconsiderate. I was warned but still dumb-struck when a visiting young Saudi Royal had me wait thirty minutes in my car when I went to pick him up at a hotel. He sauntered and sashayed down the stairs like he was walking on a cloud but the thunderbolt he received when he got into my car, was 440 Current Reality Therapy; needless to say he never did that again!

If you want to be Exceptional and produce exceptional quality work you have to be a wise purveyor of your timeliness. Time is not only money but it is also people and the opportunities those relationships are going to develop. Nothing turns someone off more than waiting for you to get your act together. You either don't know or don't care; both are fatal.

My Biochemical Molecular Engineer who graduated with a 3.9 GPA is an "perfect" example of this Beta Behavior. I enjoyed endless amusement when a European business associate wanted to meet one of the students I had mentored. He was introduced to Charles, whose level of Clarity, Precision and on-the-ball timing even exceeded the standards of my German friend. Charles's self discipline, natural intellect, quick humor and pin-point/concise answers really turned him on. One of the parameters of the meeting was that my guest would know nothing personal about the student or his family, in addition, he could not ask any such question when they were alone. The one hour meeting went on for three hours, until Charles emerged with my guest, laughing like there was no tomorrow. I, of course hand-picked Charles, for it was a sure thing that Ludwig was going to be dazzled by the fastest steed that I had in my stable at that time. He had exceeded even my own expectations.

Ludwig's monograph was 180 degrees incorrect. Charles's father was not a doctor and he was not from an affluent suburb of Boston. This meeting was an auspicious event as Charles and Ludwig's relationship grew and flowered with internships and eventually a position for a Fortune 100 in Germany. Charles's Exceptional, World Class Clarity/ Precision performs every task as a mission of the utmost Priority. This investment in personal excellence is the Golden Apple that won him a ticket out of his life of extreme poverty and social upheaval to a place of both security and distinction. The thing I endlessly delight in about Charles is how he under-promises and then over-performs, with breath-taking results; for he just loves to please people.

GOLDEN RULE

For many who address all of their interactions with a sense of Urgency, it is not a matter of possessing some cosmic and life changing gift, but, rather something as simple as treating people the way they want to be treated. This is a noble pursuit and I applaud anyone with such a good heart. Yet, the single-minded objective, to be truly noble, must be actuated in the context of designing an operative model, where this standard is mutual all the time. I like being reasonable and polite with people who reciprocate with refined manners. It is a good thing to turn the other cheek and give others the benefit of the doubt, as you hope they will follow your cue and step up to your standard. When all of that wishful thinking, like the morning dove, has flown out the window; you have to make a stark choice: to limit your interactions with this self-absorbed, unreasonable person, or to cut your losses and stop investing your valuable time into a venture that is heading for Chapter Seven Bankruptcy. I know this sounds harsh, but the fact is, these are people who are wasting valuable intellectual energy. Worse yet, they are a distraction to your Emotional Focus.

You would think that my Draconian approach would limit my relationships and circles of influence. The contrary is actually true, as the word gets around that you are not wishy-washy but have high standards. You can be as gentle as a dove or as intrepid as a dragon; it is all up to the other party to pick which lever they wish to pull…fools tread where angels fear to go!

This Dove-Dragon Dichotomy works very well in the present Wild West-OK Corral political arena which has moved from one of altruistic intention into, sadly, a Reality Show blood sport.

One individual stands high above these gladiatorial games and even though he has never been elected to public office, he may very well be one of the most influential persons in the state, as well as the national party. He is the embodiment of the Golden Rule, and from the ranks of the mighty, to the most lowly, this is the moral yardstick he universally applies. His strong grass roots philosophy is deeply entrenched in an old school, rural neighborliness that existed in times past. Telephone calls, emails and texts messages all receive a prompt and polite response no matter who you are. He is the most eccentric and refreshing man, who is beloved by regular everyday people. He represents something very special, interacting with people with the broad of social intimacy fondly remembered by small town residents. He has imparted this tenet to many Presidential Candidates; "it nice to be important but it more important to be nice."

Nowhere could the effectiveness of his leadership be better displayed than in the current presidential primary. The "Establishment" candidate, flushed with one hundred million dollars in special interest contributions, arrived on the scene, not like he was running a campaign but as if he were being hosted by the cherubim to his coronation. Reality is a jarring thing in the Granite State and feels like a frosty January morn with the mercury at minus fifteen. Needless to say, the establishment candidate did not secure the endorsement of this individual; who they dismissed as old and out of touch. Other, more sensible candidates, with their feet on the ground, sought him out.

The lucky ones who made him state chairperson, found the endorsements of hundreds of state, legislative and local elected officials. Publicly I offered my endorsement for a candidate I still have not met, for it was completely irrelevant to the equation. We were endorsing our esteemed friend's choice and relying on his judgement. His high and fair standards were the only litmus test that we needed. It does tell the tale that you get much more with honey than vinegar for He exalts the righteous and humbles the proud. This victory I savored as most sweet.

The Dynastic Presidential Campaign spent a sultan's fortune and received only a beggar's result. You would think this would be a Learning Moment, but, alas, nothing is so blind than those who will not open their eyes to see. ... they just don't get it.

LABORING OAR
THE SOLUTION CATALYST

People who do everything with a Priority have the world as their oyster. Most are early risers fueled with a passion to do some kind of magic that day. This is not an ethic that everyone shares. A constant refrain that shocks me is that this enthusiasm is not part of a disciplined, well functioning psyche but the pathology of an over-achieving, obsessive compulsive mind. Far more freighting, is the admonition that such individuals need to be on some form of psychotropic pharmaceutical as they are driving all of the "normal" people crazy.

The backdrop of this drama finds further context in our politically correct world where you cannot call someone "lazy", as this "slur" would damage their self-esteem. Instead they should be thought of as being "Motivationally Challenged." Additionally there is an Entertainment Culture that dislikes anything which smacks of being intellectual or serious; as this too damages the self-image of those who are not privileged or gifted. What perplexes me is how we went from the scholarship of the American Century and its marathon to the top, to this sprint to the bottom? The change in our national psychology is totally contrary to the necessary levels of excellence that we need to be competitive with our global partners who have emulated our standard and execute it far better than we do. The "Cognitive Gap" this has produced seriously impacts the way that Americans think about work, productivity and self advancement. While the elite in their private schools and universities fostering our diligent old school standard, (which is now that of the current competitive global standard) are still molding some of the future's best minds; the mass are left to find their own compass and fight the tide of a popular culture that is diminishing in quality with each passing year. Our competitors know that the elite levels of American society follow a well established academic success model. That is why they continue in ever increasing numbers to send their children here.

I can recall many stories of amazing students from top shelves families who soared like eagles, only have a handful of working class families who fought the dumped down popular culture, to eventually rise up as Exceptional World Class talent. I value these young leaders more highly than the Gold Spoon Children of inherited privilege, for their climb to the summit was longer, steeper and without the safety of a line to catch them if they fell.

She was first generation American from a family that started their own construction business which as time progressed, morphed into a realty company. This pull-yourself-up-by-your-bootstraps upbringing had a deep impression upon her. Gerri loved doing things right, working to be the best and would put the necessary time/attention to accomplish this. She told me that when she was young, she was a bit of a "Tom Boy". Her wide ranging knowledge was impressive. Her staff warned me that she was "Hyper". The first thought about her in my mind was," I know that I'm really going to like her."

She ran her business with the precision of a general on the battlefront. Blessed with boundless energy, she raced from office to office with a truly hands-on approach. What I liked the most about her was the Urgency that she brought to every task. She obviously believed, if you take care of the all of the small stuff; the big stuff would have no choice but to fall into place. Gerri was a most sincere and caring person with a wonderful patience for others, not infused with her jet fuel blood. I watched as her little business grew larger and its foot print spanned the globe. She was the most proud of her children, whose Aptitude they inherited and whose zest for achievement they emulated. Their steep rush to the top used to thrill me. From Honor Roll, National Honor Society on to Summa Cum Laude university degrees, her children were all a constellation of lights, in her crown of glory. Gerri was the ultimate thought leader, who does not produce followers but the next generation of leaders… she inspired us all!

PERSISTENT

Persistent is the Cornerstone Alpha Attribute. You cannot effectively execute any of the other six on an extended/ sustainable basis without it.

Persistent is the infusion of highly refined intellectual and emotion skills. In the harsh operating environment of our current world, this impetus is that little extra gas in the tank that can put you into over-drive to climb even the steepest slopes. As in the children's Story The Little Engine That Could the Persistent mindset's refrain is, I know I Can, I Know I Can, I Know I Can and when the Achievement has been won, I Knew I Could, I Knew I Could, I Knew I Could. The remarkable thing about the experience of cumulative Achievement is that it strengthens the spirit to drive doubt and fear away. As I tell all of my students, "Hard Work brings Good Results. Good Results brings Confidence. Confidence builds Experts.

This is the key thing about people with Persistence; they are far more effective than people who do not practice it. Time and time again, I observe athletes, scholars, successful entrepreneurs and a long list of ordinary people achieving extraordinary things simply because they are like that Little Engine that Could.

Persistence is a high energy, vigilant and long suffering skill of vision that focuses on extended strategic objective and not the quick win pat on the backside "that-a-Boys/Girls." All to many start off on the Exceptional Quest with the best of intentions but ultimately refuse to live the life of Self Discipline that it requires to make the journey a success. I often speak of my "High Flying Millennials" who are the top five percent of their peer group. One of the primary things about them, that separates them from their peers, is a better understanding of the operative dynamics of life. The High Flyers, unlike their peers never feel entitled to anything; they know there is no such thing as a free lunch. High Flyers follow the time honored philosophy of one of my favorite Ancient Greek sages; "If you are aiming for something high, then you will have to give something up in the pursuit of achieving it."

Persistent People know the rules of limiting their Entertainment in exchange for Achievement and denying their Self Pleasure in the course of Advancing Forward. You cannot serve two masters. You can nip and tuck at the edges of these paradigms but the High Flyer Millennial Stand Outs all follow this Exceptional Success Recipe. They discover their Truth/Talent, formulate a lifestyle recipe and then strictly follow it with repeated precision just like a twenty four jewel, world class Rolex. Like the Little Engine, their ascent up the hill begins slowly, progressively increasing in speed until with polished perfection they fly across the finish line. Those small things that they quietly do each day make them the Pace Car, while everyone else scratch their heads and ask, "What have they got, that I'm missing?" The answer is a Persistent System and Methodology of Implementation that's not fancy or complex but just consistent... Heaven's filled with the souls of the sincere, not the perfect.

HIGHLY DISCIPLINED

Every Exceptional Individual has this Beta Behavior as one of their belt loops. In fact, I've never met anyone who is Exceptional that did not have a precise and uniquely configured discipline model platform from which they worked.

My scholar athletes are among the hardest working people with whom I have ever partnered. The demands upon them are just enormous, in terms of well scheduled use of time and the energy to do all of these diverse activities well. One of the first things that I've learned to do is to create a daily To-Do List that is written a day prior to its use. The first step is basically a brain discharge of all of the tasks on the Punch List. Then, I teach the skills of prioritizing the task in relation to time needed and expectation date. This process trains the mind to think more clearly, but more importantly, lessens any anxiety as all of the necessary elements of the "Roadmap" are known upfront factors. In this manner, there are no stray fastballs coming at me from left field, especially when my gas tank is on empty.

This exercise has accomplished miraculous results. As time progresses and these twin compensating behaviors take hold, an imprinting within the unconscious, a beautiful Clarity and Self-Discipline arises. Lives change with dramatic improvement, as 2.1 GPA students now race to the top with now 3.2 GPA results.

The question that revolves in my mind is; What has changed inside that brings such a level of new clarity? I surmise it to be their new lifestyle structure slowly changing the plasticity of the brain; a biochemical reaction to the speed bumps of the self regulating mentor and personal investment of mutual interacting to achieve a high objective. This may be the case, as many of my students who were on cocktails of medications, reduce and then eliminate their usage in short order. Still more surprising, is that in the vast majority of student there is very little regression.

Once the sweet fruits of this lifestyle are tasted and all the "Endorphin Accolades" of their accomplishments fill their heads with a new form of stimulatory sensation, a new die is cast. While this is all good, staying on that path requires constant self aware vigilance. Unlike the High Flyers who do this as easily as opening their mouth to take a breath (as this behavior has become an automatic, involuntary response to them); for the newly reformed, it is a Learned Skill that requires continuous practice. Creating those new neurological connections requires experiences.

With time this Learned Skill becomes an Automatic Behavior that, just like the 24 jewel watch, knows what it is supposed to do. It then executes it precisely, flawlessly and is a valuable resource that others come to depend upon.

ACCEPTS NO LIMITS
THE INEXHAUSTIBLE SPIRIT

While mere mortals are weighted down with concerns of social convention's unwritten rules, Exceptional Individuals soar above the landscape on a unblemished canvas as vast as the blue sky. They are eccentric and iconoclastic as they do not concentrate on all of the trivia that the toxic mainstream culture cranks out non-stop.

This noise neither amuses them or annoys them. They have constructed a life that is a Golden Circle, in which they can step into the midst of the raging madness and just as quickly step back into their world of sanity. These are people which are not interested in ever hearing the word NO. Hopelessly positive / optimistic they consistently achieve greatness, while doing less and by expending even fewer resources. That's what makes them so Exceptional. Their secret lies in living life by their own rules and not directing attention to what anyone else thinks about them.

You would think that this eccentricity would put others off, but it has the opposite effect because these people know who they are and don't want to be anybody but themselves; a certain grace surrounds them. One does not have to be highly empathic to feel it, as their energy is omnipresent in such large doses that you can't help but notice.

Several years ago my parishioner at the blessed age of 111 passed to her reward. She drove her car until she was 100 years old and even received a speeding ticket. Auntie lived in her own house, with only a morning attendant and took no medication. Her cheerful disposition and bright countenance would lighten the room. When asked about her advancing old age, she was completely dismissive and looked at you like you were crazy. At 105, her children came to ask her if she wanted the security of one of those around your neck Live Line Dispatchers. She exclaimed, "You're all crazy, that's for old people!"

She live her life on a vast and endless scale, as Auntie had a very large family that by the time she was 111 was comprised of well over one hundred individuals. Auntie completely comprehended the responsibility that came with being Exceptional, and just like the Queen of England, fulfilled her role with dedicated diligence. When asked "what kept her going?", she was quick to say, "that her large family needed her!" Her passing was swift, silent and merciful, as it seemed that the Divine One needed her to continue her work, but from a new dimension. Her family were inconsolable as something precious was taken from them. The priest's homily offered thanksgiving for such an amazing soul to dwell in our midst. Several years later, people still speak of her wonder, as if her limitless energy was not of this world but of the next. The Exceptional Mind cannot be contained in a little box but its inexhaustible spirit must soar with its expansive grace that seeks to change the world.

PERFORMANCE DRIVEN
PERFECTING YOUR TALENT

Exceptional people are motivated doers who not only produce quality, but also quantity. I think of the old Yankee saying, "If you want to get something done. Give it to a busy person." My own grandmother, whose time spanned almost nine decades and lived through a life of constant changes, was always doing something. I remember giving her eulogy, in which I remarked that she was a prodigious cook, who created not just the best quality food, but had the capacity to produce an extensive diversity of cuisine in large quantities, flawlessly every time. All of this food was artfully presented, with its rose radishes, parsley wreath circles and colorful spice garnishes. Truly a spectacular display worthy of the table of any sultan or maharaja.

I need not spend a great deal of time pondering my own creative talent, as so many of our gifts are wired into our DNA. While this stream of consciousness has its provenience in my own biology, make no mistake it was further crafted through the living examples of other individuals that amplified my talent's effective usage. This all leads back to my primary theory of life. First, you have to Discover your Truth/Talent, then Create your Vision and once you become the proficient expert; Establish your Legacy.

Every Exceptional individual that I have met follows this Success Recipe. I do get a little tired of hearing that these exceptional people are just plain lucky or that someone gifted them a break. In Boston, "Tom Terrific" Brady is the closest thing I have met, in the American Psyche who is like a living god. Not being any type of sports fan, I personally don't feel the earth move under my feet at the mere mention of his name. Yet, I will admit his persona intrigues me. Is he a prima donna riding the waves of fame on his laurels?

From my observation and through discussion with people who know more of the inside element of this man, what makes him such a superstar is how performance driven his persona is focused. I marvel at his diligence, precision quality, persistence and confidence. What truly impresses me are all of the soft skills in his politeness, humility and charity. I really love how he gives back a portion of his blessing to the community.

One of the things that distresses me is how his critics unfairly maul him and attempt to bring him down. This is the dark side of the American Psyche, where we just don't want to believe that anyone can be that perfect. Sorry, Tom Terrific's process of perfection is his Success Recipe that consists of endless self disciplined hard work. While on the outside, there are those people who only see the many homes and other materialistic traps of fame, there is no free lunch, even for Tom Terrific, whose life is a study in raising your game to a world class level of consistent excellence. I am still not a sport's fan, but I think Tom Brady is a most Exceptional Individual.

SIGNIFICANT IMPACT
ESTABLISHING YOUR LEGACY

It must be my mid-life focus and the thousands of pages of speeches, sermons, topical papers, books and web content that I have banged out over the last forty five years which makes me such a student of history. From that history there emerges a deep respectful understanding of the cycle of life. We're born, we learn, we grow, we give back and then we die. Just like the Sower and the Seed; a good life is one that produces sweet fruits one hundred fold. In that process, our seed transforms and follows a well established life cycle path. It is indigenous to the human spirit, when it is awaked to the wonder of life, to leave behind a unique contribution that furthers the Treasury of Goodness. This belief in Altruism has been an essential part of human civilization's advancement. One of my greatest worries, in the present time, is that this shining gift has been subverted by those whose lust for power and greed has diminished the garment of light, that once was the ultimate prize; esteemed by all. Their unhealthy images fill the minds of a new generation. Like all young people, their hopeful optimism looks to visionary elders to color the dreams of better days to come.

For the previous twenty years I have had the privilege to partner with someone who shares this similar vision, that it is not Pollyanna to believe in a Shining City on a Hill. His steady ascent upward is like the Little Engine that Could; slow out of the gate, only to gain its rhythm to speed him onto a global stage. More than anyone else that I have ever known, this man comprehends the critical place in history that he is living through in the work that he presently performs. Just like a stone cast into the waters, whose ripples move outward in all directions, his footprint has become an annual Signature Experience, whose Significant Impact will be felt for many years to come.

At a time in America where race relations are being tested, our mutual Love of the Good flies high above the tempest below. It is this spiritual dimension that frames the thrust of his work at a time when people are looking for leadership's direction. I admire his sure hand, calm rhetoric and uplifting message, as it provides perspective that centers his audience to more productive expressions of their energy. His greatest legacy will be the thousands of new businesses and tens of thousands of successful people who found their first step up and forward by attending his annual event.

It is the highest art form of Exceptionalism, to advance more than just a self oriented personal agenda, but to be the spark that creates a movement, whose energy becomes a lifestyle; that transforms into a culture of success. In less than a generation, he has accomplished such a achievement, whose impact will ripple like that stone for many generations… In the emptying of self, we find the perfection of self … the true gift is the sacrifice that our seed must make, as it springs forth its life, to beautify the world.

ACHIEVEMENT

Exceptional Individual lives in the light of their Achievements.

All of the Alpha Attributes that motivate the many Beta Behaviors form an Operating System of many small moving parts that hum along like a twenty four jewel Swiss Watch. They are an amalgam of Natural Talents fused to Learned Skills. Cumulative positive experiences, layer by layer imprint a uniquely created Success Recipe; which is individuated uniquely to that person. It is a most complex affair, replete with numerous challenges . Thankfully, our amazingly remarkable unconscious navigating system stores all of these bits of data; like a computerized rudder, it is always compensating and working unseen in the background to keep us on course. We underestimate just how much of the learning process is unconscious. Were it not for our unconscious faculties doing their yeomen's work, no human being could ever rise to the point of perfecting the process to become what we call Exceptional.

So the Achievements that we so readily see and measure as a benchmark of success, are, ultimately the final product of a complex blueprint combining talent and effort. For me what makes the entire process so fascinating is in understanding its formation and procession.

From the essence of who we are, a uncontainable energy bursts forth, as our motivation seeks to express its creative uniqueness. This uniqueness which we would call our personality, becomes through the creative use of its energies, shapes the lifestyle we choose to live. This lifestyle becomes through its repetitive actions, the foundation of your Operative System that, through many cumulative Achievements, becomes your Culture of Exceptionalism. Everyone has the abilities to take that lump of raw Aptitude and through sheer determination forge that piece of iron on life's anvil into the shining steel of Achievement. Not unlike the blacksmith's toil ,this is an enterprise of sweat and blood, transforming your existence into a beautiful life. The hotter the fire, the more obstacles we have to overcome; the better the steel and the person that I meet.

I have always felt sorry for the children of the affluent, for despite their best efforts they are never quite the complete person like someone of humble means who arises like the phoenix out of the hot fires. These fires forge long lasting and hard won skills, which are not skin deep, but can stand the test of time with a fierce resilience that is necessary for the time in which we live. These talents manifest themselves in seven areas of leadership which are the components of this Exceptional Culture. While strengths vary, all of the Exceptional people I've encounter are proficient in all seven. In our 21st Century World, these are the seven elements, if you can master, will bring a life of excellent quality and sustained Achievement.

INNOVATION

This has nothing to do with technology, though this may be the first thing people think of when they hear the word Innovation. A delicious life of constant creative innovation is the greatest blessing that I could wish on anyone. Every day, getting up and having something in your head that's going to create "Stuff" is a feeling that is hard to describe. Even writing this book, my joy in crafting this brings such happiness all day. To the creative mind, such activities are not a chore, but a blessing. The more you create beautiful things, the more you have an appreciation for the wonder of life.

The illustrator of my series of children's books has that spark and zest which comes from absorbing the world around you, processing it internally while finding your uniquely personal artistic voice to bring it into the world. We joke about the book that we have produced together and actually called them

"Our Children". The process of collaboration and the excitement of bringing something beautiful that makes other people happy is feeling that is so difficult to describe.

Creating content in whatever form, is the Lingua Franca of the 21st Century. My partnership with these young people who are forty years my junior and who live on the other side of the planet, shares a common vision which is the global future. Their ability, not unlike my illustrator's mind's eye to take my personal expression and digitize a corresponding crafted image onto a global platform, is an assured Success Recipe. This process of Innovative Creativity is fragile, as it requires a very specific formula which demands that you listen with your heart and leave the dysfunction of the world outside of your Golden Circle. No greater blessing could I desire for anyone but to have this gift.

LEARNING

Exceptional individuals are eternally immersed in the process of Learning. Our quest on this Earth, until our final day is the acquisition of additional enlightenment. People who don't get this are missing one of the most rewarding parts of life. There is no clearer indication of an Exceptional Individual than their Learning Leadership, in the context of a Community of Purpose. This Leadership takes on a variety of forms that are as unique as each individual face.

I remember establishing an Adult Education Program in the local school district. The entire seed money and operating budget came from private sources. You would think that such a gift would be welcomed with open arms. The opposition was passively aggressive and subtle, as for anyone to criticize anything charitable is a form of political suicide. Yet, the small minds in the small town, out of sheer envy, were determined to kill this program. Mustering the collective benefit to the community, I partnered with some very unlikely allies who brought about the swift corrective action that provided the solution. The program flourished with a diversity of course offerings, and like a rolling stone gathered no moss, as it picked up an abundance of new patrons. The impact on the greater community was significant, and due to that support our Adult Education Program expanded into some professional certificates and vocational training.

Our opposition slowly melted, eventually transforming into future supporters and even, more surprisingly, patrons. Our national Exceptionalism was born out of the ascension of public education in America, which fostered this Culture of Achievement. Learning is the essential life blood that continues to renew that our path forward and upward.

Our society that is so transfixed with being continuously entertained, couple that with a politically correct culture that has obscured the necessity of merit, in labeling it as the unfairness of privilege; both have severely weakened our tradition Culture of Achievement and the American Dream. To be Exceptional is to be constantly swimming in the waters of learning, not by yourself but with a school of young minnows who you are leading upstream. This is yet another of life's great joys.

CAPITAL

Capital more than mere dollars and cents, is all about energy. How much do you have to expend to get the results that you want? This is an easy back of the envelop calculation, for the experienced in this subject. What resources must be configured to put together the effort that you will need to achieve your objective? What qualities do those resources need to possess so they can get the job done? So many people waste so much of their energy running up blind alleys, only to come to a brick wall. The Exceptional possess a certain "sixth sense", that quickly cuts through the rocks as they seek to find the diamond. So Slow down, and try to see the trees before you attempt to describe the forest. Know all of the pieces on the table before you attempt to put the puzzle together; for the learning the process is the most important learning moment.

Still more strategic is the more effective use of money which is always a value of your Talent and your Time. We created our Talent Types product with a "sweat equity" approach, that used our time as our working capital for we had the luxury of as much time as we wanted. This gave us the space to slowly build, discuss and test everything to artistic perfection. Just like the Medieval Cathedral Architects, we had both ample resources and time to develop a masterpiece of quality. Long after the cost would be forgotten, the masterpiece legacy is in that which people will see forever.... few things done quickly stand the test of time, which is the ultimate effective use of Capital.

RELATIONSHIPS

People, can't live with them, can't move forward without them. It's all a part of our basic human fabric; we were designed for each other. The wrinkle in the flesh is all of the work necessary in managing the complexity of relationships. How do you accumulate the range of sophisticated perceptive skills to sort the wheat from the chaff? Not an easy task to be sure, but one that is made more manageable if you rely on your basic instinct to do its detective work of keeping you informed with accurate information.

One of the great challenges with our Western Society's Educational Model is our strong believe in the power of Rationalism. I think, therefore I am, may very well be a statement of individual empowerment but by that assertion, it also seeks to be the predominate mode of inquiry and assessment. Long before there was the concept of the Great Social Contract, hundreds of generations followed something far more predictive; as it was built upon the instinctive wisdom of tens of thousands of years of collective human experience. One of the questions that I pose to all of my students, "What is more powerful, A Thought or A Feeling?" There is nothing stronger than a Feeling, as its impetus does not just ruminate between the two hemispheres of your mind but is an instinctive expression of your Total Self.

In evaluating all of my relationships, it is never a calculation of the mind, but an instant feeling of the heart. Has such a romanticized philosophy of human engagement clouded my rational judgement? Not at all, as this highly refined connection to my Total Self seeks to discover a single objective about the other individual; what is the motivation of their heart? Being a spiritual type of individual, that is where I connect with every one, and due to this, all the variables of race, class and age are quite irrelevant. Within thirty seconds to a minute of meeting an individual, I have absorbed their "Good Karma" and have an instant "flavor" of that individual. The level of accuracy is astonishingly high, but I must give accolades to my wife, as in the many decades we have been together, her immediate assessments are always pin-point. In fact, in nearly forty years, she has never been wrong once.

In being directed by instinct which is the dynamic physiological energy that supports your intuition, your "gut feeling" will always be more accurate than intellectually spinning all the factors in your psychic centrifuge. Simply train your mind to listen to what it feels,(this energy is the cumulative wisdom of our ancestors given to us through their hard won collective experiences). With this knowledge in your pocket, go and separate all those sheep from the goats. Success is found in making cumulative good decisions and being most particular in the circles of excellent people that are in your Community of Purpose…. Sincerity of the Heart inspires Loyalty in our Minds.

CULTURE

Your Personal Culture is Your Signature Brand; your Trademark that establishes your footprint, a mark of distinction. It is the first impression that people remember and the lasting memory that they talk about the moment you leave the room.

One cannot successfully navigate the tumultuous waters of these times with a tepid personality. More than to make a big splash or to show off, it is basic survival in the competitive environment that is not longer local or national but a global platform.

On the day of our birth, we were bestowed with our portion of talent. Our task was to shape this divine gift into something of significance. Not everything is fair. Many had more advantages than others. However it is useless to concede to the "victim culture." I think of the blessed, Mr. Kernstein, who lost his entire family in the Holocaust. More than being a "victim", he casted aside his great loss and honored his family by coming to American, becoming tremendously successful and leaving his vast fortune to an endowment that will benefit future generations. The greatest victory of the good is to take the elements of darkness and transform them into the elements of light. So when I hear people complain, I tell them the "Kernstein Story", which makes their petty concerns looks as silly as they are.

Like Kernstein, one of the great things about being a part of a sub-culture is the daily dance that you must do, keeping one foot there while the other is in the mainstream culture. It also teaches you, to develop your own Personal Culture and how important having a Signature Brand is in bringing your uniqueness into the world. Your Personal Culture is a crucible which contains your value system, philosophical beliefs and operating principles. They may morph and flex with the times but its solid core is your rock. Kernstein, knew who he was and developed his American Success Recipe which was the external expression of his Personal Culture.

From this authentic place, you move forward with strength and the shifting sands of our toxic mainstream have zero impact on your focused efforts. This focused and purposeful energy is attractive, especially to those trendy people who immersed in the flash and glitz of the superficial culture. Your Signature Brand, when supported by your creative diligence and persistence, makes you a "stand out". However the consistency of its execution is critical to your success. Your Trademark is the twenty four jewel time piece, that sweeping second hand gliding effortlessly around the dial. People notice this type of authentic confidence, knowledgeable expertise and razor sharp thinking. As I tell all of my students, "If Kernstein could do that much, then how much more are you capable of accomplishing with the big advantages that you possess?".

The future belongs to those, who know who they are, and where they're going.

EXCELLENCE

Excellence is one of those very overworked words. The mere mention of it smacks of a cliché that is tired and, ironically, uninspiring.

Consistent, best in class, excellent quality works are the hallmarks of the Exceptional individual. This high standard flies in the face of a race to the bottom in Quality, by the vast majority of people in the Mainstream Culture. I could write a complete book on the causes but for our discussion here, the results are far more important. Billions of dollars are misspent and millions of hours wasted, as our collective culture has become addicted to non-stop entertainment, that continues dumbing down our society.

Where there are great challenges, there are even greater opportunities for the individual who wishes to ascend and build a successful life of significance. We only have to recall the "Signature Experience Pizzas", and their rock solid operating philosophy of uncompromising quality, to see that such a Personal Signature is the first thing people notice and the last thing they remember about you.

People know the difference. If you want to develop a Loyalty Culture of Raving Fans, avoid listening to the crowd, as they will never let you move forward; but grab you back into the fray. The Land of Excellent Quality is a lonely road, where the mediocre minds are forever going to give you a hard time. Their envy is their challenge and ultimately their curse. Turn down the volume on that noise, cut your losses and surround yourself with people who share your quality vision. It is not easy, but I've done it, for a person cannot produce continuous creative quality, if they are distracted by this nonsense. No one may distract you without your permission. Life is short accept only the Best!

This is where your Personal Culture comes into play. You know who you are and though you may not always know exactly what you want, you'll know for certain what you don't want. Never be ashamed of your diligence, commitment to quality or your willingness to deny your own comfort, in order to achieve something great. Our entitled society has been led to believe that there is some kind of free lunch. There is not!

Sorry, but no one has ever achieved something sustainable or significant by not investing their time/ resources into getting to their destination. Even among the privileged that I know that inherited their great wealth, the exceptional and most successful work with great diligence every day. Images of them sipping champagne and eating frais en chemise on their yacht are a myth; a convenient excuse for those who wish to believe that the cause of their misfortune is the privilege of the elite, and not their own lack of self disciplined direction. Nothing is easy. To be Exceptional in today's highly competitive world requires the exertion of extra effort and a confident vision, that foregoes momentary pleasure for long term strategic results…this is the truth!

TIME

In the 21st Century, Time is the Ultimate Currency of Value to which nothing else compares. The wise management of the six other areas of leadership are necessary, if you desire to harness this uncompromising master. The older you get, the more time you have used and you begin to realize how little remains. This realization results in diametrically different reactions from people. For those who have discovered their truth, crafted their vision and have been blessed to see the fruits of their labor; they bask in the Golden Glow of their Winter Years. For those whose life has been one of indolence and many temporary pleasures, they are happily nostalgic with the memories of these experiences, but equally distressed that the time has passed so quickly. What remains for them is a life of ever declining returns; sad to say, you only get out what you put in.

How do the Exceptional/ Global Best manage their time? This is a question I have been asked many times. Of course experiences vary considerably, but from my inquiries, people who have accomplished significant achievements have given up a portion of their lives of temporary experiential enjoyment. Their joys are different, as they are derived from their families, their expertise and their achievements. All are long-term investments which require considerable hard work, worry and concentrated effort.

They are always thinking and within that thought process, always thinking about how to wisely use their time. The Exceptional are shrewd managers of time, which should not be compared to the trendy concepts of "Multitasking" in which you compress too many activities into an impossible increment of time, usually produce final results that miss the Global Best Standard by a country mile. For the Exceptional, everything is a matter of organization, preplanning and exhaustive preparation which results in World Class Quality on every occasion. It is all a part of their personalized Success Recipe.

They have a particular ease to them and are not all hyped up, overly aggressive or out of control, like so many who follow the popular culture's operating habits. I believe it is their tangible achievements that provide them with a great deal of personal satisfaction. With that satisfaction comes a strong belief and adherence to their unique Success Recipe that forms, the orbits of associates, seasons of their work and ever flowing stream of creative consciousness, that like the twenty four jewel watch; keeps doing what it does best. The Exceptional are most unaware of just how amazing they are, as this is all they know. These wise stewards of time are vigilant, having their eye on the ball all of the time and when that perfect opportunity is presented, they are ready to hit it right into the stands.

In their dedication to Self Improvement, and not shallow Self Pleasure, they gracefully age through life's seasons, delighted with the good that they do and hope that its benefits will remain long after they pass…for the final measure of the good, is in how long it will last.

EXCEPTIONAL

I will end our journey where we began. As we have discussed the various bits and pieces of this "Exceptional" ideal, which of the three examples, that I wrote about in the beginning of the book is the one that is truly Exceptional?

I've asked that question to many, and thankfully no one picked the first example of my golf experience, which was a freakish, unique coincident that will never happen again. My use of this example was to demonstrate just how Bread and Circus shallow are the motivations of the Popular Culture's thinking. My children tell me that my reaction to this is due to my lifestyle of constantly working, which make considerations of recreation most difficult for me to understand. My plight appears to be endemic with those Exceptional people. The person who makes their work their play, enjoys themselves every day. So sitting here, banging out this new creation, is delicious fun and usually the highlight of my day; not work at all.

This is one of the great challenges of all Exceptional individuals; they are so very counter culture. The Exceptional are always in a marathon to the top, while the popular culture with their addiction to 24/7 entertainment, are on a sprint to the bottom. Many compensations and accommodations have to be made, to fit in, so that these Exceptional individuals look "normal" and can function with regular people. This is not any type of intellectual elitism, but a sad reflection, for as a society, we say that we admire "smart" people, but their mere presence makes us feel inferior; as if they're judging our lack of that certain je ne se quoi. The vast majority of Exceptional people who I've met are not geniuses, but while you're living a footloose and fancy-free lifestyle, they're purposefully working; literally all the time. Regular folks are quick to tell me, the Exceptional person's workaholic habits are "unhealthy", and that this makes them are very odd.. Now who is judging who?

All of my top performing "High Flying Millennials" conceal their total gifts, especially from their peer group. It makes life just that much more simpler. As I said earlier in the book, The Land of Excellent Quality is a most lonely place.

All of my New Age and spiritual type friends picked the "Mile High" encounter with the Ivy Leaguer as an experience that was not only Exceptional, but kind of cosmic. Sorry, that's not Exceptional either, as this bestowed talent is far outside of my control. It takes all of my faculties just trying to manage these perceptions and in the vast majority of occasions, I wish that I had discovered where the "Off Switch" was located. The arbitrary quality of this ability makes it too unpredictable or undependable to be counted as a consistent Exceptional Talent.

Those bright bulbs who chose the "30k College Windfall" are correct. This entire enterprise was truly Exceptional from all sides and from every definition of the word.

This Magic Feat required all seven Alpha Attributes which were backed up by each of the many Beta Behaviors. It was the culmination of considerable organization, pre- planning and detailed rehearsal that was focused with laser accuracy on achieving a well-defined objective. It is the dynamics of taking that raw Aptitude, and, like the blacksmith on the anvil, forging it into the weapon that we desired whose spear tip precisely scored a direct hit and won the day.

Still more essential, is that this brief encounter had a long term, significant impact upon my student's life. That one hour was a life changing experience. As I stated earlier, it was one of the happiest days of my life. So, while some count their joys in attending the next party or in satisfying an itch that they have no self-control to stop, the Exceptional mind denies this type of self-indulgence to dream and achieve things that fare far beyond their own little footprint in the sand.

The path less traveled is more solitary and is one in which your good thoughts, most surely, become your best friends. To be Exceptional is to live a good, ordinary life, in which, through your passionate embrace and diligent commitment to Excellent Quality, you rise and achieve many extraordinary things.

This is not for everyone and requires a constant commitment to self sacrifice, which, as time progresses eventually becomes your lifestyle, then Personal

Culture and finally, the Legacy of Achievement of your five million moments on this planet. Once you find Your Truth and formulate Your Success Recipe, everything else falls into place. The key thing is to keep on paddling upstream; never stopping. Naturally there will be some rough currents, rocks to avoid, dips in the water and even some unexpected dunkings into the fast raging stream. Just stay on course, Let your intuition be your compass.

Every journey begins with a sincere first footstep. Never lose the zeal and good feeling of that moment when you saw your first footprint in the sands of life. It is not the intellect that creates Exceptional anything but the spirit. If you remain honest to its truth, it will take you so very far in life. Never lose sight of your creative imagination, for it is the place of dreams and the dreamers that brought the first light into the world. Each of us is a Miracle, conceived in a moment of great love and our most expressive task is to bring, share and grow that love in the world. All of the powers from above surround you and are daily working for your benefit. With this little bit of new knowledge in your pocket, make a change, do some good. The world awaits the Perfection of your Exceptional Talent, that with some sincere effort, like the frozen seeds in the cold Winter earth, will awaken to blossom into the beautiful flowers of Spring.

www.ingramcontent.com/pod-product-compliance
Lightning Source LLC
Chambersburg PA
CBHW032020040426
42448CB00006B/680